MIND FULL

UNWRECK YOUR HEAD, DE-STRESS YOUR LIFE

DERMOT WHELAN

GILL BOOKS

Gill Books
Hume Avenue
Park West
Dublin 12
www.gillbooks.ie

Gill Books is an imprint of M.H. Gill and Co.

© Dermot Whelan 2021

978 07171 9179 6

Edited by Emma Dunne
Proofread by Djinn von Noorden
Printed by CPI Group (UK) Ltd, Croydon, CR0 4YY

This book is typeset in 13.5 on 20pt Adobe Garamond Pro
with headings in Brother 1816 Printed.

The paper used in this book comes from the wood pulp
of managed forests. For every tree felled, at least one tree
is planted, thereby renewing natural resources.

A CIP catalogue record for this book is available from the
British Library.

For Corrina, Owen, Matthew and Rose.
Okay, and Buddy too!

Dermot Whelan is an award-winning radio and TV presenter, comedian, public speaker, meditation expert and midlife skateboarder. He currently hosts the popular 'Dermot and Dave' show on Today FM. Dermot is also a certified 'Masters of Wisdom and Meditation' teacher and works with all kinds of companies and organisations around the world, helping them to understand and manage stress. He likes golf, Munster Rugby and any TV show with Vikings in it.

FOREWORD

After I read this book and put it down, it had fixed whatever block I had harboured towards the concept of meditation. Meditating was something I had tried several times over the years, something I wanted to understand, but, in the end, I had convinced myself that I wasn't one of those people. Now I realise there is no prerequisite character type. It's just for … people.

Full disclosure: Dermot Whelan has been pal of mine for over 20 years now. Let me tell you a little bit about him if you don't already know him from the radio or the telly: he has always been funny. I mean funny to the point of thinking you might not be able to breathe because you are laughing so much.

He is also an excellent conversationalist, an average drummer, a dad, a middle-aged skateboarder – and someone experiencing the same stresses and pressures of being alive that we all experience. Above all, he is a generous, kind and curious human being. And I think it is that curiosity that led him on the journey that you will read about in this book.

Curiosity is something that can fade as we get older, as we do our bit, accept our lot, knuckle down to the business of life, etc., etc. But it can be a very powerful thing if it is nurtured. For Dermot, it led him to meditation, becoming a teacher and writing this book.

If, like Dermot, you have a curiosity about meditation, about how it works, and about how it can become a very gentle and helpful addition in dealing with the day-to-day, then I reckon you've come to the right place.

This is a lovely, funny, honest book. Like the fella who wrote it.

– Cillian Murphy

CONTENTS

INTRODUCTION

A year and a half ago, I was performing stand-up comedy to 10,000 people at Dublin's 3Arena. If you had told 16-year-old me that this was in my future, I would have spilled my supercan of Coke all over my bubble-toe Doc Martens. But there I was, looking out through the stage smoke at all these little heads looking back. I'd got my best mate, Dave, with me and we were on the bill with a bunch of other comedians. Ever since I'd seen Monty Python sketches as a kid, I'd dreamt of doing something in comedy. And ever since I'd entertained my family by doing impersonations of my dad eating chocolate, I'd enjoyed the feeling I got when I made a group of people laugh. But this wasn't my sitting room – it was the 3Arena! It's where I saw my first concert as a young teenager – Huey Lewis and the News. Even if they were woefully uncool, after hearing 'The Power of Love' on the *Back to the Future* soundtrack I knew I was a fan for life. In fact, I still have the badge I bought at the merch stand that night.

I never dreamt, though, that I would someday stand on the same stage as Huey and/or his News. Yet there I was, all those years later, in a position any performer would be envious of, taking in the sheer size of the venue and what it took to get me here – aaaaand it was fine. Like, just grand. Not overwhelming, not life-changing, just grand. I couldn't understand it. Little bits of wee should have been coming out with the excitement of it all, but it felt like I was in Harvey Norman's bedding section browsing for a new mattress. The set went well; they were laughing – I know because I was aware of the slight delay in the laughter coming back to me in an arena that big. But as I got into my car after the show, I remember wondering why I didn't feel any real buzz. What was wrong with me? The reason any comic does those terrible gigs where you bomb like hell and regret all your life choices is so that, maybe, one day long into the future, you might get a shot at a stage like the 3Arena. Yet there I was, driving home and already thinking about what biscuits we had in the cupboard. I had no answers to why I felt that way. Until the following Tuesday.

I was giving a talk on stress and meditation in a well-known insurance company. I was relatively new to corporate work as a meditation teacher. Sure, I had done hundreds of corporate shows as a comedian, but this was a new departure in the wellness area and I really wanted it to go well. There were 30 people there and it seemed a lot. The room was shallow but ridiculously wide, and I remember thinking if this was a comedy gig I'd have been doomed from the start. I gave my talk, and it went really well. The staff seemed to engage with what I was saying and, technically, nothing disastrous happened. I gathered up my laptop and bag and headed for the door.

As I walked out on to the street, I got this enormous rush. It was incredible. It was like every endorphin available decided to have a party and I was the guest of honour. I think I was the happiest person ever to stand on Tara Street. (In fairness, it's not a street you generally associate with happiness.) I remember being totally taken aback by the intensity of the positive feelings I was getting. Where was it coming from? This was just a corporate talk with 30 people. It's also fair to say I've never been particularly fascinated by insurance. But I realised in that moment that it was stemming from a place we have all heard about but that is rarely understood – *fulfilment*. This was what fulfilment felt like. I was doing what I always did – standing up, speaking and cracking jokes – but this time I had purpose. I had a message. I had something that people could ponder, digest and actually bring into and *use* in their daily lives. I'm not trying to undermine or lessen the power of humour for helping people when they're struggling, but I was clearly looking to communicate on a much deeper level. That day, I realised that I wanted to bring more of me to the table.

There is so much satisfaction and joy in making people laugh and feel good, but I also wanted to share some of the things that don't make us laugh all the time and to use humour to shine a light on the parts of us that we often ignore or fear.

This was why chatting to 30 people in an office gave me more of a buzz than 10,000 people in an arena. There was more of *me* present. And when we bring more of 'us' to any moment, the experience is so much richer and, well, fulfilling. A sense of fulfilment comes when we can turn up to any experience with so much of our true selves packed in there that we no longer depend on the outside world to give us what we're looking for. Sometimes, the dry ice and giant stage can be a distraction from where we're actually trying to end up – happy and content in ourselves.

I wrote this book because I wanted you to see that it takes very little to bring us to that sense of fulfilment. It doesn't require you to blow up your life and move to Nepal. Tapping into a little bit of silence within yourself may eventually lead you to quit your job and find something more fulfilling, but it may also help you to reignite your passion for the job you have right now. Breathing a bit slower and deeper could create the space for more love in your life or it could remind you that you have all you need right in front of you. Meditation is not a magic wand or a nuclear bomb. It won't instantly make you into Oprah or Stephen Hawking, and it won't suddenly flip your life on its head. What it will do, though, is ease you out of the stress response long enough for you to see what you really need.

I also wrote this book because people kept asking me to recommend a book on meditation and I couldn't really find one that I'd like to read. Some are too science-y and others are too religious. Most people just want to feel less 'meh' all the time and don't need two thousand years' worth of spiritual teachings to fix that. Of course, some of those ancient texts can be truly life-changing if you are drawn to them, but many of you just want to sleep better, not snap at the kids and feel like you can go to work without punching Leonard from Marketing.

Most of all, though, I wrote this book because I know what it's like to feel crap. I know what it's like to wake up in the middle of the night with a pounding heart and a frantic mind. I know what it's like to feel uncomfortable at work and worse at home. And if you're struggling at the moment, or feeling like you've lost touch with that happier version of yourself, then this book is for you. Believe me when I say, because I know from experience, it takes very small changes to make long-lasting differences in your life. And this book is a great place to start.

Over the next few chapters, we're going to learn about stress – why we're so afraid of it and how we can make it work for us instead of against us. In 2007, according to the American Psychological Association, over half of participants in a national stress study thought a moderate level of stress had no real impact on their physical and emotional wellbeing. Just seven years later, however, a 2014 Harvard study showed 85 per cent of Americans believed stress had a negative effect on health, family life and work.[1] In this book, you'll learn that our perception of stress is more important than stress itself, and you'll learn the techniques to shut off that inner alarm that can wear us down and burn us out.

We'll discuss the latest science behind meditation and why you don't have to realign your chakras to feel the benefits. We'll see how just a few minutes of meditation a day can:

- lower stress
- reduce anxiety
- reduce depression
- boost your immune system
- improve your sleep
- boost your creativity
- make you happier
- increase your confidence
- improve your memory
- improve your focus
- lengthen your attention span
- make you kinder
- lift your mood
- stop you freaking out when somebody doesn't indicate on a roundabout

You will also have exclusive access to my guided meditations, and I promise to use my least annoying voice when we do them. We'll look at alcohol and how it can throw you off track, and we'll examine all the other things you can do to get you back to feeling like the real you.

I promise to keep it light, and I promise you won't be living in a cave, wearing a loincloth and standing on your head by the end of all of this. Unless, of course, you like the sound of that – in which case, go for it. Maybe it's curiosity that made you pick up this book. Maybe you're looking to rediscover a part of you that has been silent for a while. Perhaps you or someone you love is stressed out and looking for answers. Maybe I know you and you're reading this to be polite so that when you meet me you'll at least have read the introduction and can then bluff your way through the rest of the conversation. Whatever the reason, I say, 'Well done!' You're already tapping into your self-awareness and that's going to go a long way over the following pages. And, as Huey Lewis sang that night in what was then The Point, 'I'm so happy to be stuck with you.' No idea of the song reference? That's fine too! Here we go …

CHAPTER 1

DON'T LET ME DIE IN MULLINAVAT!

'Really? I'm going to die here?' This was not how I'd pictured it. In fairness, I don't think I'd ever actually pictured my death. That would be weird and dark. But if there were a guy, a kind of death travel agent who showed you a brochure of loads of different types of death, this was definitely not the one I would have chosen. I would have gone for something with swords and shields and chain mail and beards and last words like 'I will die with honour for I have fought well!' (I watch a lot of shows about Vikings.) But I certainly never saw this death coming – a heart attack beside a pebble-dashed wall in Mullinavat. I doubt very much the death travel agent had that anywhere in his brochure – even among his last-minute deals.

But I was in a bad way. An ambulance was called and some people were gathering. It was in Kilkenny so they were probably holding hurleys. As I lay on the ground, gasping for air, I became aware of pillars. I was lying on the grass verge outside a bungalow and it had 'those' pillars. You know the ones – for no apparent reason, they have a giant eagle on top. They'd look more at home outside the house of Pablo Escobar than an Irish three-bed you just know has seven kinds of damp. And here I was, on its sliver of road frontage.

My hands had started to go into a twisted spasm, so I had to ask my brother-in-law, who was with me, to dial my wife's number on my phone. It was time to say goodbye. She answered, and I started to tell her I loved her more than anything I could ever imagine. Except my jaw and tongue had also begun to spasm so all she heard was 'aahhh bllleegggraaa bbblaaahnnn uuurrggghhh!' – the words every woman dreams of hearing from the father of her children in his dying moments. But the thing is, I wasn't dying. I just thought I was. I'd better explain.

***

I arrived at comedy and radio quite late, relatively speaking. I didn't get into radio until I was nearly 28, and I was 31 before I ever did a comedy gig. Most of my peers had pounded the stage in their early twenties and had inflicted the comedian's lifestyle on a body that was barely out of school and brimming with resilience. But I had spent my time in university as a wannabe archaeologist and most of my twenties working behind the scenes on film sets. So, when I was starting to gather momentum as a comedian and a radio host, I was already married with children and dealing with all the added extras those experiences bring with them.

I'm not entirely sure why I studied archaeology. I think it had a lot to do with seeing *Raiders of the Lost Ark* when I was 11. Harrison Ford was so effortlessly cool as Indiana Jones and I wanted a piece of his whip-cracking action. Pretty soon, I learned that actual archaeology is nothing like those movies. If *Raiders of the Lost Ark* had been based on Irish archaeological reality, the film would have been two hours of Harrison Ford sitting in a damp ditch beside a half-built service station – more *Indiana Jones and the Maxol Garage of Doom*. Indie, head to toe in Penneys raingear, fights tirelessly against his relentless foe: drizzle. My experience certainly wasn't all gold statues and bejewelled staves, but I did get to go on a dig in Sicily. I remember getting very excited when I found a piece of glass. It was worn and faded but light green and quite beautiful. I plucked it from the soil and ran to my college professor, who was busy sitting down and sweating.

'Look! Look! Look what I've found!'

'Well, well, well,' he said as he examined the sparkling gem. 'This really is a find.'

'What it is it? How old is it – 300 BC?'

'Close,' he said. 'It's from the 1980s. It's a piece of a 7 Up bottle. Now get back to work.'

He was a jolly Englishman, but he didn't pull his punches. He was quite overweight, lived for red wine and steak and regularly overindulged. On another trip to northern England and Wales, we were at one of the few surviving towers along Hadrian's Wall, the great Roman line of defence against the savage Celts. He was describing the history and fate of the building with great reverence and detail then, on finishing his on-site lecture, declared, 'Now, if you'll excuse me, I'm going to be sick.' And he threw up last night's dinner all over Emperor Hadrian's pride and joy. I remember falling in the grass I was laughing so much. No one else thought it funny and they scolded me for being so uncaring. But I found the whole incident brimming with comic timing and it was, in a way, perfectly fitting for a hangout for Roman soldiers. They loved puking so much, they invented the vomitorium.

Although I didn't realise it then, I had unwittingly plonked myself into one of the most mindful careers there is. The process of archaeology requires great patience as you slowly peel away history, layer by layer. Attention to detail is very much at its core and hours can pass in an instant as you repetitively sweep away at the earth. You're out in nature, deep in the soil and free from distraction. I, however, was 21 and didn't really give a shit about all that, so I smashed everything with a pickaxe. I was not a patient archaeologist at that age and certainly had no desire to explore mindfulness. I remember desperately smearing mud on a cracked

Roman pot I had just smashed, in a vain attempt to make a fresh crack look like it had happened two thousand years ago. My puking professor saw right through my scam and was not impressed.

In reality, Indiana Jones would have been fired and excommunicated from the archaeological fraternity – he was the worst archaeologist ever! He never documented anything. Not a diagram in sight. He never had permission to be there, had no respect for indigenous tribes or their beliefs, and any precious historical building he entered invariably collapsed within minutes of his arrival. Although, some of the Indie movies' sense of adventure did spill over into real-life archaeology. While in Sicily, we awoke one morning to find our van had been stolen and a chicken nailed to our front door. He was quite dead. It was a welcome note from the local mafia (cue the mandolins). Contrary to what you might think, this was not an invitation to Sunday lunch. This was an oh-so-subtle reminder that anything of value we found should be passed on to the … ahem … Museum of the Chicken-Killing, Knee-Breaking Historical Society. We sent word that the poultry-based warning had been received loud and clear and the van promptly returned. Which, I have to admit, was a bit of a disappointment. Not that I wanted to be fitted for new kneecaps, but I would love to have seen a gang of swarthy, gun-toting, shades-wearing mafiosos cruising around southern Sicily in a minibus emblazoned with 'Trinity College Archaeology Department'. Hardly the Corleone getaway car of choice …

By the end of the four years in Trinity, I had seen all the Roman earthenware pots I needed to see, so I spent the next few years as an assistant director on television and film sets. This sounded wonderfully important to my parents when I dropped home to Limerick for the weekend. They imagined that one minute I was play-wrestling with Tom Cruise at the catering truck, the next crouched over a monitor with Spielberg, saying things like, 'Let's try that on a tighter lens' or 'Screw the budget, let's blow it up again!' In reality, I was shouting at carpenters to be quiet and making tea for actors. In fact, on my first job I didn't even have a chippie to yell at. I was placed down a forest track by the director and told to 'lock it off'. This is film-speak for 'stop anything or anyone from wandering in and ruining the shot'. I stood on that track for nine days. There wasn't a hope in hell of any traffic appearing on it. It was practically a ditch. But I was new, so very eager. Each time the call of 'turn over' came over the walkie-talkie, I would shout 'Rolling!' to the trees. One day, I thought I saw a white van coming, but it turned out to be a plastic bag on a branch.

I spent five years standing in the strangest places – up mountains, in bogs, on piers, in forests, on roofs, on boats and behind doors. So. Many. Doors. For years, I couldn't watch anything on TV without thinking about the poor bloke behind the door with a walkie-talkie, who can't stop thinking about lunch. It's a strange job, assistant director – or AD if you're cool AF. Again, it seemed like the universe had placed me in a job where I was alone with my thoughts for long periods of time, as if to say, 'Well, what are you going to *do* with these precious moments of stillness and solitude?' My answer was usually, 'Smoke Marlboro Lights?' I eventually worked my way up to the rank of third AD, which allowed me to send someone else down a forest track to lock it off. That's showbiz, folks!

One day in 1999 when I was – you've guessed it – standing behind a door, I asked an Oscar-winning actor to go on set as they were ready to start shooting the scene. Of course, 'ready' in film terms is four electricians fiddling with lamps, a focus-puller sticking a measuring tape in your face, the director having tea and a bunch of extras standing in the wrong place. This actor did not take kindly to being told to go on set and – God forbid – act, so they promptly came straight back out and punched me in the back. 'Don't *ever* ask me to go on set when they're not ready for me!' and off they went to sulk in the luxury of their damp caravan. I was shocked. That was the first time they had spoken to me. They noticed me! And I was angry. Not so much about the punch but more that no one said anything to them. Like a dark episode of *Downton Abbey*, it was more or less accepted that it was OK to batter the help. I realised I had

had enough. I looked around at the people on set. Was this the world for me? Broken marriages, alcohol abuse, drug use, casual sex. Well, when I put it that way, yes, absolutely, this was the world for me … But no! I had to make a change. It was time to move on. Time to set myself free. Time to stop being a lackey for other people's creativity and to uncover my own. Time to punch above my weight, not act as a punchbag for spoilt actors. It was time to create, to explore, to finally find a job that would let my spirit soar! That's why I became … a newsreader.

OK, it wasn't the creative whirlwind I had been aiming for. But it was a start. And radio had always held a special place in my heart. I'd spent hours as a teenager making fake radio plays where I did all the voices. A lot of them revolved around *Matlock*-style court cases and made no sense. The ending was usually either a song or an explosion. Or both. But now I had a real radio job. And it wasn't with a tape recorder – it was in a proper radio studio. Well, it was a shed. But it was a shed full of opportunity. It was on the grounds of Griffith College on Dublin's South Circular Road. The radio station was Anna Livia FM, a local station that seemed to have no particular format. An improv jazz music show could segue effortlessly into a phone-in show about cracked footpaths. I had no special skills other than impressions. And I could do really good impressions of newsreaders. I knew each one's quirks and tone, pace and timing. The only issue was I knew absolutely nothing about current affairs. Like, nothing. I knew the scripts to films like *Airplane!*, *Monty Python and the Holy Grail* and *Withnail and I* off by heart, but I couldn't tell you who the Taoiseach was. I knew fairly early on, however, that this was not going to be an issue at Anna Livia FM.

The current newsreader when I arrived on my first day was a woman who had about 17 jobs, including running the place. She asked me to sit in on the news bulletin to learn the ropes, as she was tired of doing it. Anyway, she needed the time to repair the photocopier and kill rodents. The opening music rolled and she started the news. This consisted of her licking her thumb and flicking through the *Irish Times* newspaper. There appeared to be no particular order to the stories, just what caught her eye, and she'd pepper the whole thing with Irish mammyisms like 'Bless us and save us' and 'Could you credit it?' In fairness, they weren't really ropes that I had to learn, more frayed pieces of twine, but I grabbed them with both hands. *Let's face it*, I thought, *I couldn't be any worse*. The perfect motto for anyone entering the media.

As I knew nothing about the news, I robbed it verbatim off the 98FM website, which was rarely updated at the time. I would say my news was three days old at best – but, boy, did I sound good! Soon I progressed to the breakfast show, which I shared with two co-hosts, a really nice lad called Dave, who worked in the airport, and a girl called Venetia, who seemed very glamorous. We were truly awful. But it was fun and the show was ours – probably because we were the only people willing to get up at 5 a.m. for absolutely no money.

Eventually, I sent a demo in to 98FM, the very station I had been plagiarising for six months. I was called for an interview. I remember it well. The editor, John Keogh, asked me what experience I had. I proceeded to tell him I could organise hundreds of extras in a scene. I do not know how he kept a straight face. He offered me the job and, with the excited eagerness of Reese Witherspoon in *Legally Blonde*, I leapt up and shook his hand, declaring, 'Thank you, Mr Keogh, I won't let you down!' He told me years later that as soon as I got in the lift he laughed his ass off.

I liked being a news guy, even though I didn't know anything. The news bulletins were relentless – they just kept coming. I got to wear a suit for the first time, and I went to press conferences about things that confused me. But what I lacked in knowledge I made up for in blind courage. I never shied away from a challenge, even if it made me sweat like Christy Moore in a sauna. My first ever live report from the courts was utterly terrifying. It was a mind-bogglingly dull and confusing case from the Supreme Court about the European Investment Bank. Even now, I don't understand what was happening. My whole memory of that period was asking other reporters from other radio stations what the hell was going on. This was not a cool thing to do, as we were all in competition to get the story out first. But one or two were kind and gave me a steer from time to time. (Thank you, Jonathan Healy. You saved my bacon on many occasions.)

On this particular day I was due to give a live report on the main lunchtime news. That and the five o'clock bulletin were the big ones of the day. It was a chance to prove myself as a reporter, and they were counting on me to bring them the big story from the courts. I stood outside the Four Courts with my notes and my phone, ready for the call.

At 12 noon, the call came in: 'We're going live to you in three minutes – stand by.' I could feel the nerves but was poised for action. 'We can cross live now to the Supreme Court where our Dublin reporter, Dermot Whelan, has the latest.'

Off I went. 'The three judges said today that they were –' All my notes, which I had balanced on the roof of a car, blew away. Cue white panic and flop sweats. 'Eh … the judge said … ehm … that the case … ehhhmm … Back to you in the studio!' And like in a movie when a renegade cop takes the law into his own hands, I was put back in the office behind a desk, where I could do less damage.

If you had asked me at that time if I suffered from anxiety, I would have laughed. No way! I was Dublin's answer to Clark Kent – beautifully dressed but always mysteriously missing when anything really important happened. Sure,

I got nervous and sweated a lot, but I presumed that was probably because I loved pints and cigarettes. I sweated more than anyone I knew. There were clothes I couldn't wear because of the threat of the terrifying sweat patches of death. Grey T-shirts were an absolute no-no, and I regularly sat at functions absolutely sweltering but too afraid to take my jacket off. My only saviour when out for the night was a toilet hand-dryer with a moveable nozzle – one that I could point into my pits to dry them at source. Then I could stroll from the pub jacks with the confidence of a Gillette man.

I remember doing an audition for a drama school in Manchester shortly after university and I sweated so much my yellow linen shirt (I know) turned a completely different colour. The other auditionees were just staring at my sweat patches, which crept out from my armpits and spread like a science experiment. I flopped. The college staff went into a room, had a chat and gave me a second chance. I was worse. I was just a ball of panic and sweat, even though I really wanted to do the course. It was a resounding 'no' and I set off home for Dublin. Even then, had you asked me if I had issues with anxiety, I would have said no. I just thought my sweat was caused by hormones and that it wasn't my day. I didn't see that anything was holding me back. I had accepted that, in life, some things make you sweat and panic and freak out and get dizzy, and then they're over and you have a fag.

But there was something going on with me. I was a socially anxious person. I guess I always had been. But I had no awareness and no tools to deal with it. Eventually, it would have me at the side of the road saying goodbye to my wife, Corrina, for the last time into a Motorola Razr. (They were cool phones, weren't they?) Don't worry, I'll get back to Mullinavat.

But with all these new experiences in the world of radio came more pressure, more moments out of my comfort zone. And, as a result, my body started to do weird things.

The sweating was one sign that I was experiencing stress. My voice was the other. About a year into my work in the newsroom, I went into the studio to read the news. I was sharing the bulletin with the news editor and it was going fine until it came to my turn to read a story. My voice started to disappear. It was the strangest thing. It was as if an invisible hand was choking me. My voice just wouldn't work. It started to go squeaky and croaky at the same time and I sounded like a cross between Yoda and Gollum. My boss didn't know what was happening and neither did I. He took over and I just sat there, perplexed. Afterwards, he asked me what had happened and I said I didn't know. I remember feeling embarrassed and confused. I laughed it off and said I'd be fine the next day. But I wasn't. It happened again and again. Eventually, I had to sit out the bulletins because I just couldn't trust that my voice would come out.

One of the common symptoms of anxiety is a tightening of the throat. I had no clue. And, again, I had no tools to deal with it, even if I had known. It was my normal and I just got on with it. I pushed through and soon I was able to go back into the news booth. When I think of me back then, I have enormous sympathy for that young fella. He was trying his best to follow his dream to work in radio but was swimming against the current for much of it. It's not that we can't overcome things like anxiety with a sort of mental brute force, but it takes enormous effort, and we're more likely to reach for things such as alcohol or sugar to give us a hand. It was clear my poor adrenals were screaming for a time-out but, for now, they weren't going to get one.

CHAPTER 2

STAND UP AND FALL DOWN

Doing breakfast radio is like that show *Total Wipeout*. I like to watch it with my kids. Overly confident, bubbly types take a run at an insane obstacle course designed to trip them up and, no matter how many times they take a run at it, it never seems to get any easier. In radio, there are days when you feel like you win, and inside you celebrate like a triumphant, mud-spattered contestant. But then the next day can put you on your backside again. It's a relentless, never-ending quest for content and it gallops along like an out-of-control stagecoach.

In 2002, after two years in news, I was offered the job of host of the 98FM breakfast show. This was not normal. The most presenting I had done was the odd overnight graveyard shift, which was mostly pre-recorded. But I had been staying back after work and using the newsroom computer system to record fake news bulletins with really weird characters for my own amusement – I was a big fan of shows like *Not the Nine O'Clock News* and *Brass Eye*. Soon, the late-night talk-show guy started putting them on his show and they got noticed. Then my boss at the time heard them and thought it was time to give me a break. Next thing I knew, I was brought into a room with a guy called Dave Moore and told to 'get on'.

It was like one of those painful play dates you had as a kid. We chatted away about how weird it all was. Dave had been selected as my co-host, but they hadn't told him. He didn't even know why he was there. He was a music producer who did the odd voice-over, and they just told him to come in for a meeting. After twenty minutes a woman popped her head round the door and asked how we were getting on. 'Fine,' we said and off she went again. Turned out Dave could do a rather fine Alan Partridge impression and he earned my instant respect for that. I was a big Partridge fan.

Over the next few days we were given a series of tasks like something you'd do at Montessori school. They had brought in an outside producer who appeared to be leading the charge on everything. She was either a genius or a complete bluffer. We were ordered to cut things we liked out of magazines and stick them to the wall in a sort of mood-board collage. We had never-ending brainstorms, where it was decided that we should play all our own jingles with actual instruments. Live. In one meeting, this same producer wrote the words 'God Squad' everywhere. She was adamant that we should do this as a segment on our show. It was a sure-fire winner. I asked her excitedly what it was. 'I don't know,' she said.

A week or so later, we were on the air on one of the biggest stations in the capital. We hadn't a clue what we were doing. I was pressing all the wrong buttons and doing my best impression of a 'dee-jay' voice. The idea of playing our own instruments live in studio was, unsurprisingly, not a great one. I fell over my drum kit regularly and the whole thing sounded chaotic. We were then given another producer, who would listen from outside the studio and shake her head and cover her face when we were talking. For a brief while we had a lovely woman called Aideen on the show with us. She was an actor and also had no experience of radio. In one of the early shows, instead of doing the traffic, she freaked out and hid under the table. She was gone by the end of the week.

That first year was like a tour of duty: little or no sleep, a terrifying four live radio hours from 6 a.m. to 10 a.m., and afterwards we would have all our bad bits played back to us and told we were crap. Our show was experimental and strange and we were starting to have fun, but it was clear that the people in the background had little or no faith in us. It looked like the end of the road. Then the ratings came out. We were number one. We were the biggest breakfast show in Dublin. We had toppled our opposition and brought the whole station to the top of the ratings pile. And that was it. I was hooked. We had tasted victory and we wanted to keep on going.

Radio is an amazing medium. I've done bits and pieces of telly over the years and it doesn't compare. Radio is instant. In radio, it takes one person five minutes to conceive and execute a great idea. In television, it takes thirty people six months to ruin a good idea. But the instant nature of radio can be exhausting. It's like those Buddhist monks who spend weeks creating elaborate sand paintings and, as soon as it's finished, wipe it clean and start all over again. It's performance after performance, day after day, and if your head isn't in the right place you begin to burn out quickly. Even though I was succeeding in this new field, I was riddled with self-doubt, tired and so hard on myself if something didn't work. I needed to change the pace. I needed to slow down and take a breath. Did I listen to that inner voice that intuitively knows what is best for me? Did I feck! I took up stand-up comedy!

If you ask a stand-up comedian what makes them jump on a stage, very few will be able to tell you. They just know that they need to do it. They can't help themselves. It's like when you know there is a packet of jellies somewhere in your kitchen, and, try as you might to ignore them, you will find yourself returning again and again to their sweet fizzy goodness. (Haribo Tangfastics are my sugary Achilles' heel.) You'll also find that a lot of stand-up comics were altar servers in their local church. If they were Catholic, of course – if they weren't, that would have been just weird – although it wasn't unusual for people of other faiths to join in our Sunday proceedings.

I remember, as a child, being at Mass one Sunday in our local school in Limerick. We had no church, so the Mass happened in one of the school prefabs. At this point, I feel the need to reassure you that you are not reading *Angela's Ashes*. Anyway, halfway through the blessing of the Eucharist, the school telephone rang – one of those piercingly loud landline phones that you hear blaring on old episodes of *The Bill*. The priest answered but there was nobody at the other end. This was the first of many prank calls into Mass by the local Protestant messer. The priest hung up the phone and said, 'That was the Holy Spirit on the phone!' Everyone laughed in that 'the priest just made a joke' kind of way. It was the talk of the prefab for weeks to come.

But it wasn't just the gas craic-ery of the prank calls that led me to be an altar boy. It was the fact that Mass was the only stage in town. There were no theatres. There wasn't even a town. Just Roxboro National School and a guaranteed packed house every Sunday morning. It even had its own wardrobe department and costumes. You got to wear the strange robes and hang out backstage (behind the prefab), and there was even a backstage rider – we got to eat as many unblessed communion hosts as we wanted. The priest didn't know, of course, but we had competitions after Mass to see how many pieces of round unleavened bread we could fit in our mouths at the same time – 47 is the answer, by the way, and, yes, the title is still mine. You think one communion host sticks to the roof of your mouth? You should try 47.

Each week it was more or less the same line-up on the bill – my best friends, Donny and Ed, and myself. We would take turns with the jobs like bringing up the water and wine, lighting the candles and holding that weird brass plate under people's mouths when they received communion. Ringing the bell was the big one, though. This was essentially like closing the show. It was a lot of pressure but exhilarating, nonetheless, because there was always a chance, if you didn't do it right, that you would shake the bell but nothing would happen. The audience – I mean, congregation – would look at you, expecting a bell, and you would just be there flicking your wrist madly with panic all over your face. 'Do this in memory of me …' Nothing. It was the religious equivalent of dying on your hole. The priest, who was obviously the MC, would scowl at you and you wouldn't get to close for another month, until everyone had forgotten how much you stank. It was a good training ground for performance, plus you got to scan the crowd for hotties who you fancied.

Twenty years later, I was doing my first stand-up gig in the International Comedy Club in Dublin. Comedian Des Bishop ran the club with his brother Aidan, and had offered me the open spot after hearing my late-night radio sketches. I declined because I was terrified, but he said in his broad Queens, New York, accent, 'You're already booked in. You're doin' the fuckin' five minutes.' So, there I was, December 2004, about to go on stage in a proper comedy club – and it was packed. In fairness, it only takes about a hundred people to fill the place, but most are standing and it has the edginess of a football terrace with none of the class. The walls are painted black, and it looks like it was burnt down but never repaired. It's so small, there's no need for a microphone, which generally freaks out most visiting foreign comics because they don't know what to do with their hands.

As the regular MC, Des stood up and began to introduce me. I was standing in the thick of the audience. My heart was beating fast and my stomach started doing somersaults. I was clutching my guitar, which I was going to use to close my act. Corrina was doing her best to reassure me that it'd be fine. I had all my material learned off. *What if someone heckles me while I'm on?* I thought. *What if a Protestant rings the phone?*

'Ladies and gentlemen, please welcome to the stage a brand-new act, Dermot Whelan!'

It was now or never. Just as I began to walk to the stage, Corrina, who was as nervous as I was, pulled me back and said, 'Don't do the song!'

'What! Why?' I said. 'It closes my act!'

But the pats on my back were pushing me towards the stage. I was riddled with self-doubt. I started my act. I got a laugh. Then another. Then more. It was going really well. It felt amazing! The laughs kept coming. I saw faces smiling and looking happy. It came to the song. I'm not sure which one it was, but I think it was about chocolate bars. I did the song. It killed. My time was up. They cheered. I got off. More pats on the back. I've never won a proper cup final with a team, except for the Under-12 East Limerick GAA football final against Caherconlish, which I'm not sure counts. But I imagine it feels something like this. A sense of overcoming, of achievement, of winning over the crowd and my fears. It was amazing. Even better than Mass! I learned so much about myself in those five minutes. (OK, it was more like twelve – I went way over.) Most of all, I learned to listen to my wife about absolutely everything – except what to put in my set.

I'd never felt a rush like it, and I wanted more. What most new comics don't realise, though, is that, in a way, the first gig is the easiest. Your family and friends are all there. You've prepared like crazy and you're totally psyched up for it. You're not looking beyond this gig: you're just focused on this one task, on surviving it. It's the shows months down the line, away from your support team, in a terrible room with a tiny, uninterested crowd – they're the tough ones! And, in fact, they're the ones where you really learn about yourself. They're the ones where the self-doubt is the loudest, where you really hear how you talk to yourself in your mind, where you'd give anything for a prankster to ring the phone and rescue you from the torture. Summoning up the courage and self-belief to try anything new and challenging is impressive. Hanging on to that self-belief when it really matters is the game-changer.

* * *

If this were a film, you'd now see 'Nearly three years later' fade up on the screen, along with an aerial view of a navy-blue Mercedes driving along country roads. Inside is a hungover, nervous comedian, fresh from a row with his wife. He stayed out boozing far beyond the time he'd promised, and he's smoking cigarettes and drinking organic lemonade to try to bring himself around. You've guessed it, it's me!

I'd decided it was a great idea to go white-wine day-drinking the afternoon before a major comedy festival at which I was fortunate enough to be performing. The Kilkenny International Cat Laughs Comedy Festival is a world-renowned event that attracts the biggest international names in comedy. Bill Murray has played there, Michael

McIntyre, Peter Kay, Dom Irrera, Tommy Tiernan, Dylan Moran. And this was my third year running to be asked to perform. I was silently freaking out as I drove because I knew the hangover was going to make it even harder to perform, to find that mysterious zone every performer relies on. My brother-in-law was with me and I didn't want to let on that I was having a confidence speed wobble. In an effort to keep it together, I was talking to myself like a 1930s American gangster attempting to calm down his hysterical wife when she hears the cops are on to them.

Suddenly, I started to feel strange. I picked up the bottle of lemonade and began to examine the ingredients label as if this could be the cause. Forget the booze and fags, it's the organic vanilla essence! I started to feel worse and it seemed to be coming from my stomach area. The best way I can describe it is that it was as if an invisible man had crept into the car and sat on top of me as I was driving – like you used to sit on your dad's lap pretending to drive. I could feel this inexplicable weight on top of me and, at the same time, I had a weird feeling all over my body. Do you remember those old televisions? Remember when the channel wasn't tuned in, and you'd get that black-and-white fuzz on the screen? The kind that used to communicate with the little girl in that movie *Poltergeist*? Well, imagine that fuzz has now replaced all the blood in your body. It's like a disturbing, energetic fizz that's everywhere.

I started to mooch around in my seat, open the windows, turn up the radio, but nothing was helping. The pressure on my belly started to move up my body into my chest. Now I was really getting worried, and I thought about pulling the car over. Pretty soon, I was struggling to breathe and I definitely had to pull the car over. Yellow bungalow, grass verge, pebble-dashed walls – you'll do.

Aaand here we are again. Lying beside the eagle pillars. Gasping for breath. Clutching my chest with contorted hands. And making the noise of a newborn calf down the phone to my wife. I was vaguely aware of the ambulance arriving. I heard the phrase 'suspected heart attack' and they spoke to me in those overly pally tones that you know they learned in 'emergency school' but were still very soothing. My brother-in-law didn't know what was happening, and neither did I. I tried to crack a nervous joke but, between the mouth spasms and the oxygen mask, it failed to land.

They put me in the ambulance and I was whisked off to Kilkenny Hospital. I noticed just how loud the siren was when you're inside the ambulance. It kind of added to the anxiety of the whole experience. I thought to myself that, instead of a siren, they would be better off playing ambient dance music or one of those pan-pipe tunes you hear in health spas. It would be far more reassuring and calming. I thought how strange it was that, of all the ambulance sirens I'd heard, this one was for me.

I arrived at the hospital and they hooked me up to monitors and wrote things in charts.

'We're going to have to give you something to get you through this,' they said.

What could it be? Morphine? A quadruple bypass? A last will and testament? And then they presented me with the piece of life-saving equipment – a brown paper bag. Now, I know the HSE is in trouble, strapped for cash and understaffed, but surely they could do better than Centra's finest! What was I supposed to do? Bring my clogged arteries home in it?

'Breathe into it,' they said. 'You're not dying. You've had a panic attack.'

OK, that sounded better than a heart attack or a stroke. But what the hell *was* a panic attack?

'Do you have a stressful job?' they asked.

'I'm a stand-up comedian.'

'Oh, I see …'

Any normal person would have gone home, considered their life, made lists, reached out, looked within, rested up, calmed down or, at the very least, gone to bed for a few hours. Nope. I pulled the heart monitor cables off my chest, got a cab into town and, within an hour, was performing a stand-up show in a club. Followed by another stand-up show. Followed by a load of pints and not much sleep. Followed by the same thing for two more days. One of the things I remember about that night were the other comedians who quietly confessed that they too had experienced a panic attack. Why had I never heard of these things before? And why was everyone having them?

A panic attack is basically your nervous system screaming, 'Enough is enough!' They can appear out of nowhere for no obvious reason and have all kinds of symptoms, like nausea, dizziness, numbness, tingling, a racing heart and difficulty breathing, while all the time you're thinking, 'Jesus Christ, I'm dying!' I can't explain how terrifying it was. They can also cause you to hyperventilate, which had happened in my case. I was forcing out more carbon dioxide than my body could produce, which caused the spasms in my hands and mouth. Hence the newborn calf.

There were probably a lot of smaller signs that my body was giving me before I reached that point but, clearly, I hadn't been heeding them. So, how *did* I reach that point? Why didn't I just stop? Well, why don't any of us stop? Because sometimes it just seems easier to keep going. We get caught up in a relentless momentum, like those mad bastards that chase wheels of cheese down hills somewhere in England before dislocating their spines in a heap at the bottom. We don't stop because it all becomes a kind of life soup, filled with awkward things like not wanting to let others down, pushing yourself, feeling a sense of duty, seizing the day, having the craic, putting food on the table and maximising your potential, all floating in a pot of 'I'm not sure why I'm doing any of this.' We are conditioned to keep doing, keep earning, keep striving, and that's great – until you're breathing into a paper bag that you know had tuna sandwiches in it quite recently. So, sometimes, if you're still ignoring the warning signs, the universe steps in and gives you gentle nudge into an ambulance. I would love to say that everything changed at this point and the panic attack proved to be my transformative 'Road to Damascus' moment. Unfortunately, there were more medical emergencies to come. Anyone for karaoke …?

CHAPTER 3

THE KARAOKE STAIRS OF DEATH

One of the great things about working on the radio is the free stuff. I get sent the most random things: dog bowls, cupcakes, balloons, home-grown cucumbers, hilarious mugs, socks, DNA tests, wooden spoons, kombucha, colouring books, air fresheners and thousands and thousands of USB sticks. But I also get invited to things and, when I had more energy and fewer children, I went to everything – gigs, launches, parties, press conferences, premieres, matches and festivals. I even got a personal tour of a crisp factory, recently. I took my mum, who has dementia. She loved it. Conveyor belts of crisps whizzing by and sorting themselves into piles and falling into flavour powder. Fun fact – a computer measures the density of the crisp and, if it doesn't match the desired dimensions, a blast of air blows the offending crisp into a giant vat of reject crisps. *Pffffft!* And it's gone. We ate a great deal of reject crisps on the sly. We felt devious, like Charlie Bucket and his grandpa in Willy Wonka's Fizzy Lifting Drinks room.

I also get invited to lunches. At least, I did back then, when the Celtic Tiger was a big stripy lush and boozy lunches were de rigueur. Even when the recession hit, some event companies were still giving it social socks, and one January day in 2010 I was invited to a la-di-da lunch in an ooh-la-la restaurant. Three years had passed since the Kilkenny incident and, after a brief period of minding myself, I had soon fallen back into old familiar patterns. Steaks were seared and red wine flowed like insults in a Gordon Ramsay meltdown. Having been up since 4.30 a.m. for the breakfast show, I was feeling the benefits of the full-bodied Bordeaux and, afterwards, I retired to the pub where my friend Ed and I drank some pints and then sojourned to the street where we practised the ancient rite of the honourable day-drinker – wrestling on the road. At this point, one would think it was time for a home-cooked meal and an early night, but there was something far more important to be done before I went home and snored beer breath at Corrina – karaoke!

Karaoke is brilliant. There are few places where it's socially acceptable to shout as loud we want. A karaoke booth is one of them. Belting out songs with a best mate, that you listened to together back in the day, is a special thing. It's so much fun that we're even willing to forget that the communal microphone, held together by twelve different kinds of masking tape, is positively fizzing with bacteria. Who cares? I'm singing 'Sunday Bloody Sunday'!

We arrived at the Japanese restaurant and met the owner, who was having an anniversary meal with his wife. He offered us a glass of champagne and we chatted. I really didn't need the champagne. I don't even like the stuff, but I think a lot of us just like holding it because it makes us feel grown up. Soon, our name was called. Our booth was ready. Our audience (the wall) awaited … Ed excitedly went down the steep stairs that led to our underground stage. I followed and … well, that's just it. I don't remember much after that. I remember the sound of myself tumbling head first down the stairs, but not the actual tumbling. Harsh, echoing slaps and thuds. Uglier than they make it sound in the movies. Apparently, like any Irishman worth his salt, I managed to hang on to my champagne glass right to the very end – until I hit the wall at the bottom. Then I stuck it in my forehead and knocked myself unconscious.

When I woke up, the first thing I was aware of was the sound of a hen party belting out 'It's Raining Men' in the booth nearest me. Perfect. It literally was. I'm sure the sound of me 'raining' down the staircase just added to the back-beat. Ed was there and lots of other feet. I'd spent about a minute out cold, according to the bystanders, and I didn't really know what was going on. There was a lot of blood on the floor but it didn't really compute that it was mine. I struggled to my feet and went into the bathroom. There was a large gash on my forehead and blood all over my clothes. 'Cool!' I remember saying to my reflection. Hello, concussion. Clearly I needed medical intervention. The poor owner of the place abandoned his lovely wife and drove me to the hospital in his classic Mercedes. I remember promising not to bleed all over it. I arrived in a haze and received twenty-something stitches. I now have a scar that would give Harry Potter a run for his money.

In a wonderfully Irish turn of events, the nurse who stitched me up said he was finishing his shift and offered to drive me home. He said he lived near me but I know he was lying. He was being caring and generous and he wanted to keep an eye on me. We find fault with our country a lot of the time, but our days are full of incredible people and moments like that. In the car on the way home, I felt confident that I was keeping spirits up by chatting knowledgably on all kinds of topics. We arrived at my front door and Corrina opened it to see the blood-soaked walking wounded. 'Keep an eye on him,' said the kind nurse. 'He's been talking gibberish and repeating himself all the way home.' Oops, seems I misjudged the quality of my car bants … I fell into bed. I slept. My wife didn't.

In the bath the next day, everything was sore. Everything stung. I had a black eye, aches and pains, and a very bruised ego. I looked in the mirror. The guy looking back at me seemed like a stranger, with a strong vibe of Mickey Rourke after a proper beating. Just what was going on with me? Why was I in this state? In this bath? I knew I was drinking too much but I didn't think I was an alcoholic. Was I?

Something felt very out of balance and I didn't know what to do. I was trying my best to keep everything afloat: my job, my family, my money, my ambition. I thought I was doing a pretty good job. So why was I here, feeling like this? I started to think that I didn't fall down those karaoke stairs. I was pushed. I was pushed by the same invisible hand in my back that pushed me through every day and didn't care how exhausted I was. The same hand that volunteered for everything, regardless of how many other things I had going on at the same time. The hand that reached for red wine instead of a duvet. I thought how lucky I was that I hadn't broken my neck. And I knew I had to change something. And I would. I could feel it. But first I had to go to a cabbage festival in Germany. You're probably picking up by now that it takes me a while to learn a life lesson.

So, there's this thing in Germany called *Kohlfahrt* (pronounced 'coal fart', which is, perhaps, something miners experience). It is a festival of … well, cabbage or kale. It is a tradition of the Bremen area and sounds like the kind of event Irish people wish they had invented. On any given Saturday in January or February, a bunch of friends will gather in the countryside. They pull something called a *Bollerwagen*, a type of cart, filled with an assortment of coloured schnapps, whiskey and any other booze that is deemed fit. Everyone wears a shot glass around their neck and is instructed to fill it, based on the activity that's in play. The cart is dragged around the roads and neighbours arrange wacky games to be played en route. Everything ends in drinking. The whole day is organised by the *Kohlkoenig* and the *Kohlkoenigin*, the cabbage king and queen (bear with me), and they preside over all the activities, especially the grand meal at the end. The entire community gathers in a local hall and eats the *Kohl* (cabbage), and a weird meat called *Pinkel*, one of those foods that you feel it's better not to ask what it's made of. Everyone sings traditional *Kohlfahrt* songs and then, you've guessed it, more drinking!

In my life, I've only met one other person who has heard of this German tradition. He's an American who happens to be married to a German woman from Bremen. Everyone else just looks at you like you've mistaken your Rice Krispies for ecstasy tablets. In fairness, I had never heard of it either until the winter of 2010. My wife's brother had lived there for a while and his old buddies invited him and us back for a bit of much-needed *Kohlfahrt*ing. I was due to go the week after I had fallen down the stairs, so it wasn't the highest priority on my list. I needed to sort my shit out and I couldn't imagine a psychiatrist recommending this as a bona-fide therapy.

'Dermot, you've clearly been through a lot. What you need is space, time and quiet to heal your body and mind and, eventually, work out what's really important to you so you can take positive action to move towards a higher level of fulfilment. I recommend drinking multicoloured liquor in the German countryside with a bunch of cart-pulling strangers. Here's a prescription for some cabbage and disgusting meat. Same time next week?' But the flights were booked, babysitters were lined up, people were excited and, even if I wasn't fighting fit, my fear of saying no to anything certainly was so, a few days later, I was on my way to the airport.

As I wandered around the heavily perfumed duty free, I began to feel quite optimistic about the whole affair. Or maybe that was just the concussion. I was still quite dizzy and, come to think of it, probably shouldn't have been flying. Also, my black eye wasn't so much black any more but had graduated into a more colourful presentation in the guise of a piss-poor YouTube eye-make-up tutorial.

As we sat at our gate waiting to board the plane, all was well. Until I heard words that no one is ever excited to hear. 'Oh my God, what's happening to your face?' A quick dash to the gents' toilets revealed the cause of their alarm. Presumably as a result of the fall, fluid was filling the area between my eyebrows and spreading into the centre of my forehead. Before my eyes, I began to take the form of a werewolf who had strong ancestral connections to members of the Klingon empire. I looked utterly demented. And, horrifyingly, I had no idea how far this would go. I also had no idea if it was a sign of something more serious going on in my head after the fall. I did the only thing I could do. I harnessed the ancient wisdom of the Irish and uttered the timeless phrase perfect for any emergency – 'Sure, it'll be grand.'

I boarded the plane and hoped for the best. As I passed the air stewards, I wondered if they would insist on putting me down in the hold with the other creatures in need of quarantine. Or maybe they'd run me through the metal detector again to see if my Wolverine claws were a threat to passengers. As the wheels lifted and we headed for the home of *Pinkel* meat, I stared out the window and wondered where all this was leading me.

When we met our German hosts, two bubbly twenty-something girls, they were bemused by the man-beast that greeted them at the door. I explained, naturally, that I had fallen down the stairs, received twenty-odd stiches and my head was swelling dangerously fast, but reassured them that I was 'up for it'. To add to the overall look, I had a large white bandage on my forehead over my stitches. My hair was quite long and werewolf-y at the time, so I attempted to conceal the bandage with my fringe but it didn't really work.

Kohlfahrt was wonderfully bizarre and the German locals were so welcoming and generous. Many were surprised that we had come so far to sample this unique tradition but, as

Irish people, our curiosity for other cultures often brings us to these strange places. And if it involves booze, we tend to be first in line. There were challenges and rules and walking and drinking and it was fun. I was putting on the bravest face I could. I joined in the special and bizarre *Kohlfahrt* games. But as I threw a walnut into an egg carton held by a German, I realised my heart wasn't in it. Even the heady mixture of concussion and schnapps had failed to smooth my edges and I knew I couldn't sustain this way of life. What was I doing there? Why wasn't I at home on my couch, watching DVDs (or whatever we watched in 2010)? Maybe it had something to do with an evil nun.

CHAPTER 4

THE NUN ON THE END OF MY BED

've always had bad hangovers. Not that I ever felt too awful physically, but emotionally I was a train wreck. Even in university, when you're supposed to be able to brush off a hangover with nothing more than a shower and a Berocca, I found I always had more mental anguish than most of my friends. I didn't need Nurofen: I needed a parish priest. My friend Eddie used to call it 'grehhh', based, I believe, on the kind of sound you make when you hold your head in your hands from despair. It's also referred to as 'the fear', which eventually became so bad for me that I used to get 'pre-fear' – additional fear in advance of a session that you know will cause you to have great amounts of 'the fear'. But I loved the craic so I did it anyway.

I've always been a happy drunk and, long before I ever worked in comedy, the performer would emerge after a pint and I'd make it my mission to entertain anyone around me.

I was never a 'climb something really high' drunk, a 'punch someone in a chipper' drunk or a 'wake up in a cowshed' drunk – I was giddy and excited and friendly. Which made my reaction to the night out the next day all the stranger.

My eyes would open the next morning, I would realise that I had partied and stayed out late and then it would begin – an internal berating that seemed to be coming from somewhere inside me but separate from me at the same time. And so harsh! From the tone that I'd be using in my head, you would swear I had punched a guard, stolen his car and driven through the window of Brown Thomas shouting, 'Up the Ra!' It was self-loathing, guilt, shame and worry, all served up in a pint glass of regret. Anyone who has done three days of a festival can probably relate to what I'm talking about.

In an attempt to describe it to someone once, the nun emerged. I found myself giving these feelings of guilt and negative self-talk a persona – the nun on the end of my bed. It was as if, each time I was hungover, a nun was sitting on the end of my bed waiting for me to wake up. I imagined her sitting there with her arms folded, judging me silently. Then, when I opened my eyes, she'd say something like, 'So, you decided to wake up?' And then the negativity would follow. 'Why couldn't you have come home earlier?' 'You'll be wrecked for the day now.' 'This is all you need.' 'You won't get anything done now.' 'What kind of way is this to live?' 'You could have been up running this morning.' 'You look terrible.'

I have no idea why it's a nun, by the way, and I know it seems creepy and weird, but it helped to give the fear a personality. Perhaps it was some representation of piety or judgement in my subconscious, an authority figure that gave a voice and gravity to the criticism. Maybe my dislike of the film *Nuns on the Run* had manifested as a living nightmare. Whatever the reason for me deciding on that image, one thing was clear. I was in the habit of some very harsh self-criticism and the alcohol was making it louder.

In her brilliant book *The Positive Habit*, clinical hypnotherapist Fiona Brennan says, 'if you suffer from anxiety, drinking too much alcohol is one of the cruellest things you can do to yourself.'[2] Why is it cruel? Because the effects of alcohol amplify any negative thinking patterns meandering around your brain. Without the cloaking device of happy hormones like serotonin, which is obliterated by booze, those thought patterns run riot, and for me it was unbearable. So if I suffered that badly afterwards, why was I drinking in the first place? Well, because alcohol is also an anaesthetic. And just as it has the power to turn up the voice of our inner critic, it also has the power to, momentarily, turn it down.

I have a friend whose dad says all babies should be born with half a pint on board. And I get it! Babies would be way less cranky! In that half-pint sweet spot, the edges feel smoother and things don't seem so serious. And it became apparent to me that this was the place I was chasing. By the end of the week, I had built up so many negative thoughts about myself that alcohol offered a chance to make them silent for a while. Of course, I was never aware of what was going on when I was busy falling down staircases – it was only after, when I began to really examine my behaviour. Developing a Klingon forehead will do that to you …

I looked at why I was caught in a never-ending circle of escape and self-loathing. I gradually started to realise that if you allow your thought patterns to go unchecked, it creates a sort of imperceptible din that builds and builds until, somewhere in your subconscious, a voice says, 'I need some serious relief from this.' And, like a bubble emerging from deep in the water, a thought rises to the surface of your thinking and up pops the suggestion: 'I think I fancy a pint.' It wasn't a desire for the actual drink; it was a desire for some mental silence or, at the very least, distraction. And a lot of us follow this pattern of behaviour, this periodical numbing, because we don't have any other tools to hand. No one ever taught me any skills to deal with unhelpful or destructive thoughts. Even when I ended up in an ambulance, I still didn't know what to do. It's wonderful to see these things being taught in our schools now, but in my day, as the oul' fella says, dealing with stress or anxiety was not a thing we studied.

The closest thing we had was home economics, and all I learned in that class was how to bake inedible cupcakes and how to clean a brass door knob. Although, once, I did make an exact replica of the Karate Kid's white outfit, complete with the iron-on transfer of the setting sun on the back. It was a thing of beauty. I wore it once and it fell apart.

But deep breathing, intention setting, gratitude, the power of the brain or visualisation were never on the agenda. Mr Miyagi taught me more about focused thought than 13 years of school ever did. So, when I had negative thoughts in my head, I didn't know what to do and, as for so many of us, the chatter became normal over time until those thoughts had moved in for good.

For me, it was a constant feeling of never doing enough, of never being enough. If I was succeeding at one thing, I'd be worried that I should be succeeding more at something else. I had exceptional courage for trying something new but no faith in myself to keep it going. Stand-up comedy terrifies the bravest of souls and public speaking regularly rates higher than death in those 'Things That People Find Scary' lists. Being on stage taps into one of our deepest fears as humans: the fear of being ridiculed and rejected by the group. It's a primal fear that many find too strong to over-come. I was willing to get up there and give it a shot and risk the embarrassment of dying on my arse.

I remember doing a parachute jump with a friend of mine, Cathal Murray, who is also a stand-up comedian. We flew up in a tin-can airplane, which felt so unsafe that jump-ing out the door at 10,000 feet was a relief. We screamed like hell. Although the sound of the wind on the way down is so terrifyingly loud that you can't actually hear yourself scream. Then our parachutes opened and we floated down peacefully the rest of the way. It's a bizarre experience that goes from a feeling of 'OH MY GOD I'M GOING TO DIE JESUS HELP ME WHAT HAVE I DONE AAAAHHHH!' to 'Well, this is quite pleasant – what a beautiful afternoon.' As we picked ourselves up off the grass in the field we landed in, we both agreed that, as scary as it is falling out of a tin of John West at 10,000 feet, it wasn't as terrifying as stand-up comedy.

So, to get up on stage and tell jokes I had written had required considerable bravery. But without self-belief, that courage is unsustainable and, instead of getting easier, it can get harder and harder. Imposter syndrome kicked in and I started to entertain thoughts like *I'll be found out, this can't last* and, my personal favourite, *the other comedians are* real *comedians*. Instead of enjoying the process and gift of entertaining people, I would have a knot in my stomach for days before a gig. It would take incredible willpower to psych myself up for it, and then I'd need a drink to calm the adrenaline down after it so I could relax enough to sleep. Throw in a 5 a.m. start on the breakfast show the next day and it was head-melting.

I also had a powerful fear of failure or even making a mistake. Radio-presenting is seat-of-the-pants stuff and the live nature of the medium leaves you quite exposed. Mistakes will happen and you have to be OK with that. Sometimes those mistakes are your fault, sometimes they're someone else's or maybe it's a piece of misbehaving equipment that causes your heart to beat faster. But no matter what happens, there'll always be another show to do and you have to make peace with the mistakes and keep going. I, however, hadn't got the email on that and did not handle errors well. If I made a mistake, I gave myself an incredible lashing. We all strive for perfection but, at some point, we have to realise that it's an unattainable goal and, to continue the unnecessary football analogy, any shot on target is good enough.

A mistake for me, however, was very hard to take and, instead of letting it go and moving on, I would let that feeling fester for the rest of the show. It would naturally affect my performance and, sometimes, it would colour the entire rest of my day. My self-talk of 'you idiot!' and 'bloody typical of me!' would be bouncing around my brain and I'd have myself convinced that people were turning off their radios in droves. Apart from my unhelpful thinking, I had also failed to see the true reality of radio listening – while presenters think that listeners hang on their every word, in reality, half the time they don't even know what station they're listening to!

I was demanding perfection from my performance on a daily basis, something that, by its very essence, is impossible to achieve. There are just too many variables. Perfectionism of any kind, in any job, comes from the same place – a feeling of not being enough. It says, 'If I make just one mistake, people will see that I'm not up to this task and I will be found out.' Sometimes, our perfectionism becomes so intense that beating ourselves up is no longer enough. We then feel the need to have a go at the people around us.

One example of this is the petty tyrant. Ever work with one of those? Someone in a position of authority who compensates for their lack of self-belief by constantly attacking others. Robert Downey Jr captured this in a Joe Rogan podcast recently: 'Being self-critical is important. As long as it doesn't bleed out into the people around you and make everyone miserable.' Iron Man said that, so it must be true.

Criticising yourself is exhausting. It demands all your attention, all your focus, and you become self-obsessed. And it's actually quite conceited, when you think about it, as if the future of the world depends on how you perform at work, relationships, sports or whatever you happen to be doing at that moment. American author Carlos Castaneda wrote, 'The fatal flaw is that average men take themselves too seriously … What usually exhausts us is the wear and tear on our self-importance.' We can get so tangled up in our own thoughts about ourselves, and what we should and shouldn't be doing, that we gobble up all the oxygen and energy available to us and, when that's not enough, we begin devouring everyone else's.

One place you can witness negative self-talk is a golf course. I like to play golf. I've played since I was a kid and it has a magical effect on my mood. It's sport, meditation, mindfulness and craic all rolled into one. Corrina was not always a fan. In fact, on our second date, I opened the boot of my car to get out a bottle of champagne and she noticed a set of golf clubs in there. 'Please tell me they're not yours,' she said. It transpired that later that evening she rang her mother to fill her in on the new guy. 'Well, what's he like?' her mother asked. 'He's lovely but … he plays golf.' 'Ah, well, I'm sure you'll meet someone else.' They were horrified! Thankfully, she got over the fact that I like to hit a white ball as hard as I can and chanced a third date.

But have you ever played golf or any other game with someone who trash-talks themselves? It is such an enormous buzzkill. They huff and puff and blame and scoff and it engulfs their entire presence. The behaviour makes them antisocial and they become incapable of truly joining in the experience. So they spend their time shouting at themselves or apologising for their poor performance. In their heads, they feel like they're being thoughtful, letting you know that this version of themselves is unacceptable and they will continue to demand better. But, in reality, when we berate ourselves it is actually quite a selfish action. We are caught up in the haze of criticism and, when we're in that state, we are unable to appreciate the things or the people around us.

The angry golfer does not have time to congratulate you on your amazing shot. He or she is too tied up nitpicking everything in their environment. And usually, the rage and upset turn gradually to a silent sulk because the process is just too exhausting to maintain. A sheepish goodbye and another apology and off they go, swearing to never play again ... until next week!

If you want to see how someone talks to themselves, take them golfing. It's a magnified mirror of real life. One of the first things I noticed about myself when I began meditating was how I changed on a golf course. It seems like a silly thing. But I was that angry golfer. Not the kind that breaks clubs over his knee or, like one man I know, flings his clubs over a wall. But I was very vocal in my admonishing of myself. I would shout 'Idiot!' if the shot wasn't good and regularly berate myself in the third person. Negative self-talkers love the third person! 'Dermot, you clown! What was that?' 'C'mon, Dermot, this is pathetic!' And then I started meditating and, whether it's your intention or not, meditation fosters self-kindness, and it becomes very hard to speak to yourself negatively. So my language on the golf course softened. Suddenly, I was not beating myself up as much, so I had the time and attention to be truly present with the people playing with me. It's not that I no longer cared where the ball went or how I played – I cared just as much. But I was able to channel my energy into actually concentrating and improving rather than swearing at myself and slamming clubs into bags.

And this is what was happening in my head before I had the tools to do something about it. I was wrapped up in self-critical and anxious thinking and was clearly suffering from what I like to call 'a terrible dose of the "shoulds"'.

'Should' is a dangerous word. It's a bit like a virus and can spread through our thought patterns without us being aware of it. Shoulds are the thoughts that emerge when we feel we are not doing enough, we are not being enough. How many of these have you had today?

- I should have got up earlier.
- I should have gone to bed earlier.
- I should be less tired.
- I should exercise more.
- I should drink less.
- I should do more with my kids.
- I should do more for myself.
- I should see my friends more.
- I should eat less.
- I should be skinnier.
- I should be stronger.
- I should earn more.
- I should be doing more.
- I should get more fresh air.
- I should *be* more.

A should, every now and then, can be positive. It can gently nudge us in the right direction and spark improvements in areas that possibly need some attention. 'I should pay my credit-card bill before I get charged interest.' 'I should take my car to the garage for a service.' These are helpful suggestions that could make our lives easier in the long run. But if the shoulds change from being intermittent to all the time, the landscape of our mind becomes a very unwelcoming place – a place where the only satisfied inhabitant is the nun on the end of your bed. As the shoulds pile up, we begin to feel overwhelmed and helpless. There are too many things to deal with at once. The scale of importance of each one becomes dysfunctional and 'I should look younger' takes up the same room as 'I should leave my job'. They look for spaces to emerge in your thinking. They love nothing more than when you feel inferior and start comparing yourself to others. 'I should have that many followers on Instagram.' 'I should work out as much as him.' 'I should have a car like that by now.' The shoulds make us feel sad and then we 'should' about the way we feel. 'I should feel happier.' 'I should feel more grateful.' 'I should feel more in love.' 'I should feel confident by now.'

They love to come out and play in the middle of the night. Ever have one of those nights when you wake up and go through a mental shopping list of all the things you should be doing more of, less of, better or differently? As

I write this, I'm thinking I should be writing quicker! The problem with a should is that it suggests a sense of urgency but offers no obvious solution. It can feel like warning lights flashing on your car dashboard, but as soon as you try to deal with one, another one grabs your attention. They are always there in the background but it's up to us how much space and power we give them.

In this book you're going to learn actual techniques to tame your shoulds. And you'll begin to notice them. You'll begin to know which ones are important and which are unnecessary and unhelpful noise. The spaces between them will get longer and longer until they barely register in your awareness. And, hopefully, the only should thought will be 'Shouldn't I have had more shoulds today?'

Chronic 'should-ing' can lead you to a point where you're no longer able to enjoy life because you're caught up in reaching the next thing. That could be burying yourself in work or obsessing about the gym. We've all met the triathlon king or the ironman queen who started out just trying to get a bit fitter but soon became expert in trapping you in mind-numbingly dull conversations about 'personal bests' and 'sub two-hour' whatevers. Just because you look good in Lycra doesn't mean you're immune to the devious power of the shoulds. And this is what was happening to me when I was burning myself out. I felt I should be the king of radio, television, stand-up comedy, corporate entertainment and, let's not forget, karaoke. There is no reason why I couldn't be all of those things, but why did I need to conquer them all at the same time? When was I supposed to sleep or rest or spend time with the people I love? And I mean quality time, not time where I'm walking around like a zombie. Because shoulds don't care about rest or downtime. They see it as a waste of perfectly good time that you could be spending out there striving, achieving and getting!

Don't get me wrong – there is nothing unhealthy about having goals and ambitions. Used in a healthy way, they can be exciting, motivating and give us an enormous sense of wellbeing and fulfilment. But we have to give them the patience and respect they deserve. We need to be thoughtful and prepared and driven by the pure excitement of reaching our goal. Remember the movie *Rocky*? One minute he's pounding joints of frozen meat with his fists, then he's skipping up the steps surrounded by a group of children who seem very excited about a man in a tracksuit. That cheesy montage is a great example of quiet, humble preparation that doesn't lose sight of the innocent excitement that makes reaching a goal fun and worthwhile.

But when our ambition is driven by a fear of not achieving, of being left behind or missing out, our careful planning and strategy go out the window. Our approach can become frantic and directionless, and we end up saying yes to everything in case we miss the 'golden opportunity'. It's more like a blindfolded treasure hunt than a well-planned mission, and all that running around in circles can leave you feeling utterly depleted. One of the added downsides to suffering from a serious case of career FOMO is that you often end up working for crap money. As fear is your driving motivator, you regularly undervalue your worth and experience because you're afraid you'll miss out on the 'big one' or offend someone in authority. This is where you fall for magic beans like 'it'll be great exposure', 'it could open a lot of doors for you' or 'you'll be working with the right people'. If they were the right people, they'd pay you what you're worth!

There will, of course, always be times when you work for free or for very little because it's a passion, a hobby, or you're trying to get something off the ground. Maybe it's a stopgap on the way to something better. If it's a part of a plan fuelled by excitement then go for it. I, however, was in a pattern of thinking and behaviour that put me last and everything else first. I was a yes-man to striving for the sake of it, which meant my way of living was more out of balance than Mr Blobby on Jägerbombs. The reasons I was standing there, concussed, throwing walnuts into an egg carton in Bremen were the same. Fear of missing out, fear of letting people down, fear of actually sitting down and asking myself, 'What do I want?'

CHAPTER 5

TIME TO CATCH MY BREATH

'It's about a woman who makes lingerie.' Some weeks had passed since the fall and German cabbage had become a distant memory. My head had healed, except for the Harry Potter-style scar left on my forehead, which acted as a constant reminder of the danger of mistimed karaoke. The fall was still on my mind and I knew I needed to find something heavy on self-belief and light on head injuries. I was having a conversation with a woman I'd just met who had written a book. She lived in Howth, where I had recently moved to, and she was full of life. Her name was Siobhán McKenna and she wanted me to host the launch of her new novel, which was based on a woman who worked in the clothing industry. I'd never launched a book before and I thought it would be a nice way to meet more people from the village, so I said yes and we started chatting.

It turned out, not only was she a writer, but she was also a meditation teacher. This seemed like more than just coincidence. This could be it. I had heard of meditation but assumed it was for hippie types who have beads instead of doors. But she seemed so … well, normal, and she was also clearly very creative and successful, so there had to be something in it. In fact, she taught stressed gardaí to chill out, which seemed like some achievement. 'Can that be my payment?' I asked. 'Can you teach me how to meditate?' We agreed on the barter and it set me on a path that would literally change my life – or, rather, how I perceived my life and everything in it.

The first time I tried meditation I was embarrassed by the word. I remember saying it to Corrina and feeling myself blush. 'I'm going upstairs to medi … *mumble, mumble.*' I thought it sounded so pretentious. It wasn't what Irishmen said. We should be saying things like, 'I'm going upstairs to bleed the radiators,' or 'I'm going upstairs to hide from your mother.' But this suddenly sounded so 'Californian' or like something Gwyneth Paltrow might say as she carefully lit a vagina candle (she really sells them). It was one thing trying meditation, but to say it out loud seemed, to use that most effective of Irish words, 'wanky'. Thankfully, my wife was into this stuff long before me so she really couldn't care less. In fact, she is always a fan of me doing anything that puts a smile on my face and gets me home before 2 a.m. Uninjured.

I had been given my instructions by Siobhán, which included something called a mantra. This is a syllable, word or phrase that you repeat silently in your mind. I later learned that 'man' comes from an ancient word for mind and 'tra' represents vehicle. Literally, 'vehicle of the mind', which is pretty cool. Or, if you're a garda, 'veh-hicle of the mind'. The mantra, I had been told, had something to do with the alignment of the stars and planets at the moment I was born, but I didn't quite understand that part and pretty much just nodded through the explanation. All I knew was I was supposed to keep it a secret. It seemed reasonably exciting, in a kind of *Goonies* sort of way, so I went with it.

I sat in my office chair upstairs and closed my eyes. I began to repeat my mantra over and over again. I became aware of my breath and the silence in the room. My mantra continued in my mind, again and again and again. And then, after a few minutes, it happened. NOTHING. Literally nothing happened. I'm not sure what I had been expecting. Maybe some colours? A vision of a past life? A voice of a deceased relative? 'Deeerrrmmmooottt. Weee aaalll sseee whaaat you dooo iiinnn the baaathrooommm …' Nothing.

Any films I had seen about meditation masters usually led to waking up in another dimension or, at least, to some very impressive martial arts. There wasn't a nunchuck in sight. Had I missed something? All I felt was a bit more relaxed and slightly more aware of my breathing. And this is what I was to learn – it's supposed to be underwhelming. We're not supposed to feel … eh, whelmed.

We are so conditioned to expect an immediate response or result from our actions that we are disappointed if something doesn't deliver straight away. If we get in the car, we move. If we lie down, we fall asleep. If we sit on the couch, we see the telly. If we eat a meal, we become full. If we meditate, we hear ourselves breathe. That's it.

Now, there are a lot of things happening in your body and brain that you will be unaware of, and we'll get to those. But to your busy, 'thinky' self, it seems like nothing is going on. And, through a bit of practice, we learn to be OK with that. It's what starts to happen over time that will keep you coming back for more. And you will probably have a hard time describing why or how you feel better but you just do. You know when you vacuum your sitting room and everything just feels and looks nicer? Like, how much dust could there really have been? You didn't actually do that much – you just rubbed the hoover over the thing – but the whole room seems to be cleaner and tidier. Even the air in the room seems lighter. Meditation is that – a vacuum cleaner for your mind. After a while, you'll forget about the hows and whys and just settle into this new, happier you.

My personal trainer, Ronan Murphy from Toned Fit gym (who is seriously suffering from neglect), says this about his clients who are frustrated about getting results in his gym: 'Reading body language and postures is a large part of my work. When a client has started into a new training programme, they can sometimes feel like they're not seeing results. A lot of the time, however, and unbeknownst to them, they're already standing taller and more confidently, almost from the first day!'

Meditation is the same. You won't be the first to notice anything different. It will be something someone else says *to* you. For me, it was my wife. She remarked on how much more patience I had with the children. Not in a 'it's great that you don't beat the kids any more, Dermot' kind of way. It was about how I was acting in that 6 p.m. to 8 p.m. kids' bedtime window, where all parents' patience can be tested.

It's a tricky time for a lot of people. You've been working hard all day, in or out of the home, the children are at their giddiest and/or crankiest and you know that, once your little darlings are tucked up under their My Little Pony duvets, Netflix and possibly a glass of wine await. Or at least a biscuit. A few months into meditation, a different, calmer, more patient version of me was turning up to bedtime. I wasn't so uptight, so parent-y, so 'come on, get into your pyjamas and stop the messing!' My dad voice was softening and I was laughing more. Now I was the one messing and play-fighting and making up stories. In fact, one of the characters I came up with during a particularly giddy bedtime is soon to be a book – but that's literally another story. And isn't it funny how when you're less cranky the kids are too? And it's then you realise how much those around you feed off the kind of energy you're bringing to the table.

Maybe this bedtime lark has never been an issue for you, or maybe you don't have children and have yawned your way through the last paragraph. Well, just think of a time in the day or any instance when the prickly version of you comes out to play - that reactive, impatient, triggered person inside you that often regrets how he or she has behaved or spoken. Now imagine that, with just a few simple exercises, you could smooth those edges and sweeten the experience of you being around for the people you love or spend time with. Wouldn't you consider trying something new?

The next people who remarked on this new and improved me were my work colleagues. I realise I'm beginning to sound like a type of washing-up liquid (*new, more powerful formula!*) but bear with me. My co-host, Dave, and I have been working together for more than eighteen years. I've easily spent more time with him than my wife. In fact, our wives call us 'work wives'. He knows *everything* about me. And I him. He has seen me at my award-winning best and my absolute worst. He knows that I unnecessarily slept in a bath after the Radio Awards one year, and I know he collected fancy paper as a teenage boy. We have witnessed the birth of each other's children – well, not actually witnessed, but you know what I mean. We can pre-empt each other's moods and predict each other's next sentence by the raising of an eyebrow. So, if anyone could detect a change in my behaviour, it would be David Moore. Remember the 'Oh my God, you idiot!' moments in the radio studio from before? Well, he was the one who pointed out to me when they disappeared. OK, he would probably step in here with a point of order, so perhaps I won't say 'disappeared' – maybe 'considerably lessened'!

Something else that began to change after I started meditating was my desire to drink alcohol. It's not that I suddenly became a monk, but I noticed the idea of going for pints or opening a bottle of wine just wasn't as appealing. Because I was giving uncomfortable emotions a chance to be processed through meditation, I guess I didn't feel as much need to reach for the numbing effect of booze.

I was also getting used to being in a happier state. As soon as I had a drink – or worse, a hangover – I couldn't wait to get back to my normal mood. I used to really enjoy the alcohol buzz, but I was beginning to find it uncomfortable and weird. More than that, it began to feel unnecessary. So I found myself reaching for a non-alcoholic option or avoiding the pub altogether. I didn't become a teetotaller but something in me had definitely shifted. I believe that many of us are more emotionally affected by alcohol than we realise. I'm not anti-alcohol but I believe that many of us are indoctrinated in the cult of booze at an age when we are emotionally vulnerable and our brains are still growing.

Drinking can be an automatic behaviour that we take on without ever really getting a chance to understand its effects or the reasons we feel we need it. If you think you wouldn't mind reaching a point where alcohol plays less of a role in your life, then rejoice in the fact that you're reading a book that has already helped set you on that path. I will come back to this subject later as I'm dying to tell you what I learned from my grand booze experiment!

But what did this change in my behaviour actually mean? My not freaking out showed I was less reactive. This would also suggest I was more in control of my emotions. I was taking more time to decide how I was going to respond to something. I was being kinder to myself. My negative self-talk had lessened. You could also argue that my belief in myself had increased, as I didn't feel the need to punish myself for mistakes. And, I'm sure Dave would add, I was nicer to be around and easier to work with. Not a bad result from one change in behaviour! And that is what my teacher, Davidji, refers to as your 'ripple'. One small adjustment in how you respond to your actions or environment can ripple out in an infinite number of ways to the people and situations around you.

I was in Spain a few years back on a holiday with Corrina and the kids. By this stage, I was spending at least twenty minutes meditating every day. On the first day of our trip, we drove to the beach. It was a textbook Spanish afternoon on the sand – paying extortionate prices for sun loungers, screaming at the children to put on sun cream and Corrina trying to talk me out of buying everything the 'lucky lucky' lads have to sell. (I once bought a pair of Nike Air Max from them. The Nike symbol came off in my hand.)

Anyway, I decided to go for a swim to cool off. While I was in the water, I felt the wrapper of a chocolate bar in my pocket. Except it wasn't a chocolate bar wrapper. It was the key for the rental car. I had brought it swimming by accident. The reason I didn't notice it in the traditional 'I'm about to go swimming' pocket pat-down is because some eejit at the Renault factory thought it would be really clever to design a car key that was as flat as a credit card. I mean, seriously, what's the point? I really don't feel the need to start my car like an ATM. And, funnily enough, immobilisers don't function well when they're soaked in salty sea water so we were properly banjaxed. (What is it about rental cars that strikes the fear of God into the hearts of the strongest warriors? I can even imagine Paul O'Connell's hand trembling at the rental desk as he murmurs, 'No, I don't want the full insurance, *gracias*.')

So, here I was at the beach with a sodden novelty key and no way back to the apartment. Being Irish, we had brought four thousand plastic beach games, wind-breakers, chairs and cooler boxes, so walking was not an option. I called a taxi, which arrived and promptly drove off again because he didn't want to get sand in his car. I'll be honest, that tested me, but I kept my head. The worst part of all this saga was that it was me who'd caused it. Like many dads, I'm the one who preaches about where to park the car safely, who says, 'Christ almighty!' if someone slams the car door and shouts, 'Easy! Easy!' when the suitcases are going in. I keep the rental forms in a clear plastic folder and hold all the passports because no one else can be trusted. I rant about 'these bloody rental companies', and every father worth his salty keys can list off at least five car-rental horror stories he has picked up along the way. But now, here I was, dangerously close to being another Joe Duffy holiday-disaster story. It was only a matter of time before I had a thick northside Dublin accent, saying things like, 'Joe, dem caaar rentil companeez are a diz-grace!' My only option was to leave our crap in the rental car, call another cab for the family and get yet another taxi to the rental place at the airport, pay for another key and pay for another fare back. I was looking down the barrel of €400 at least.

At this point, old Dermot would have called himself every name under the Spanish sun for swimming with the key. Then I would have gone for the sand-phobic taxi man. And the journey to and from the rental office would have been less craic than Castlebar the day after an All-Ireland football final.

But none of that happened. After the momentary shock of realising what I had just done with the key, we all laughed our asses off. Corrina didn't let the delicious irony of me being responsible pass unnoticed, but it was *funny*. I had no idea what we were going to do but it didn't matter. I knew I was going to work it out. The money was a pain but we had enough to cover it and I was grateful we did. (No, insurance doesn't cover key sea swims.)

Once the family was safely delivered home, I was happy and quite mentally prepared for the cab ride to the airport. Instead of being miserable, I was upbeat and chatted to the taxi driver in one of those classic Spanglish holiday conversations. 'Oh, si, los irlandeses, muchos çerveza, ha! ha!' And get this, he enjoyed my company so much, he only charged me one way – €75 off! I arrived home with a huge smile on my face and we headed for the pool. On foot. And, of course, years later, any time there's a lull in the conversation or I'm lecturing the family about not locking the back door, out comes the holiday story. 'Remember that time Dad went swimming with the car keys?'

This may seem like a trivial tale, hardly life-changing – but that's the point. Our lives are made up of lots and lots of tiny insignificant stories, incidents and encounters that are hardly Pulitzer Prize-winning by themselves. But those moments add up, and how we act and react in those instances shapes how we see those experiences and, as a result, how we view our lives. When you put them all together, a small shift in perspective *can* literally be life-changing. It changes how you see your life. Now, I'm not saying that we need to pretend everything is fine when it's not. It's important that we feel the things we need to feel, and painting on a smile in the face of adversity is not the answer. But having the mental and emotional space to pause before it all kicks off can stop us from disappearing down the rabbit hole of negative emotion and, as a result, we will tend to spend less time reacting and more time dealing with whatever has been put in our path. Or our swimming togs.

After those early awkward meditation sessions, I continued to do it daily. I brought my new calm-inducing wisdom to many other situations in my life. I began to say no to things more often. I walked away from TV shows that were draining me. I pulled back on my stand-up comedy performances but spent more time doing improv comedy because it excited and energised me. I stepped away from the people who were sapping my energy and moved towards those who made me feel nourished when I saw them. One incredible side effect of acting in a truer way towards yourself is that, suddenly, new opportunities arise from nowhere. It's as if the higher version of yourself says, 'OK, you've stopped pissing about and you're ready for this next bit now,' and new things reveal themselves. In my case, in 2014, after years in a Dublin radio station, I was offered a shot on Ireland's biggest independent national station, Today FM. Dave and I took the chance and we headed to the lunchtime slot to do our thing. In just over two years we were handed the prime-time mid-morning show, something that would make our hero Alan Partridge very proud. 'Back of the net!'

When we free up space in our heads, when we remove the obstacles we invariably put in our own way, like self-criticism, second-guessing, self-sabotaging and any other word with a hyphen, we free up space for new things to come in. Did you ever have a conversation in the kitchen and suddenly realise that you'd left the extractor fan on? Or have you been in a café and – one of my pet peeves – the barista has left the coffee grinder just grinding away? When the noise is allowed to stop, everything seems easier. The conversation is clearer and much less work and, as a result, a far more enjoyable experience. I was finally clarifying what was important to me and doors were opening everywhere.

So how, with all this knowledge, did I end up a basket case again?

CHAPTER 6

BECOMING A TEACHER

In 2017 I sat on the edge of my bed with my head in my hands. I was so tired, I hadn't the energy to stand up. I wondered how I was going to get through the morning, never mind a national radio show. It felt like someone had turned on an energetic tap and all my essence had been pouring out of me for days. It had been another crappy sleep where I had awoken at my usual worrying time – 3.10 a.m. For no apparent reason, I had begun to wake up at ten past three in the morning and start thinking about EVERYTHING. Big or small, each thought would take up the same room, and round and round they'd go. In the middle of the night, there is no perspective. Something that wouldn't raise an eyebrow in the afternoon can feel like the end of the world in the dark. Add to this the worry that you won't be able to get back to sleep, and the following day will be a jet-lagged nightmare. You are literally not sleeping due to worrying about not sleeping. It's ironic and painful. I would lie there thinking about the alarm going off until eventually it did, and getting up was often a relief, just to end the cycle of negative thinking.

During the day, I would pray that I wouldn't bump into people in the street as making chit-chat was torture and it took all my effort just to keep my game face on. If I had a meeting later in the day, I would have to build in a nap in my car beforehand or I wouldn't be able to stay awake for it. I tried to boost my energy by keeping fit, but the workouts depleted me so much that I would be flattened for days, so I stopped.

Work was enormously difficult. Any job is next to impossible when you're burnt out but one where you're expected to uplift the nation is head-fuckery of the highest order. I had just started the new morning radio slot and was writing a live stage comedy show at the same time to take on tour with Dave. I hadn't planned to be doing both, but the tickets had been sold when the radio-show opportunity arose. Developing a radio programme is exceptionally intense and, as well as all the new ears tuning in, there is also a lot of internal pressure to make the thing work. You tend to be shown a lot of coloured graphs, and terms like 'market share' and 'daily reach' come up a lot. Fans of the previous presenter usually become very vocal and worked up on social media, and there are always murmurs of people within the organisation who feel you shouldn't have got the gig or that it's destined to fail. Or both. So the pressure is tangible.

Add to this the expectations behind our first live comedy tour as a radio duo when, as far I know, it had never been done before in Ireland. And this was no live podcast recording. This was a balls-to-the-wall insane mix of characters, stand-up, sketches, music and improvisation that tested every performance skill I had ever learned. Oh, yeah, and Dave had never done live comedy before. I felt a lot of responsibility to carry the heavier load of performance and also to keep an eye on him, as I had pretty much talked him into it.

It would be a testing time for any human. But I was the meditation king! I was tooled up with everything I needed to survive this, right? Like Keanu Reeves in those John Wick films, I should be able to flick a button in my mind and the wall of my brain would slide back to reveal a massive arsenal of stress-busting weapons perfect for any challenging occasion. So why was I gripping my steering wheel in the car park, terrified of going into the office? Why was I constantly walking around with a turbulent mix of rage, anxiety and deep, deep sadness in my gut? Because I wasn't using the things I had learned.

There's a scene in a John Wick film where Keanu Reeves takes a sledgehammer to a concrete floor in his basement to reveal weapons and treasure he buried there because he felt he didn't need them any more. But now circumstances have changed, so he digs them back up and goes to war. With mental and emotional wellbeing, you don't get to do a John Wick on it. You can't just bury the things you've learned under concrete in your basement and dig them up with a sledge hammer when the shit hits the fan. You need to channel Mr Miyagi. You've got to do your mental 'wax on' and 'wax off' so often that it becomes part of your unconscious coping strategy. But that's not what I had been doing.

I had unwittingly become what Davidji calls a 'crisis meditator'. I enjoyed talking about meditation, sharing tips, reading books and listening to podcasts, but I wasn't actually doing it. Not regularly, anyway. I would dip in and out, and maybe on a Saturday morning I would try a guided meditation. I might do three days in a row and then leave it for a week. Obviously, this was enough to keep me ticking over when things weren't too hectic, but when a perfect storm of work and pressure arose, I wasn't equipped. Smashing open my weapons stash was too little too late. Think of the gym. If I talk about fitness, hang around with trainers, listen to podcasts and do the odd 10k run, I'll feel like I'm living the life. But if someone suddenly asks me to do some 100-kilo deadlifts, I'll collapse under the strain. It's the same thing with training your mind. We do the work not just to navigate daily challenges with more ease but so that when the big things come our way we are emotionally and mentally ready. As a great sage once said, 'Bean by bean, we fill the sack.' Over time we create our own resilience built on our own internal personal training and self-belief.

I spend a lot of time in Lahinch in County Clare. I love the place and have been spending holidays there literally since I was born. It's a surfing hotspot and people come from all around the world to take on the Atlantic waves. In fact, I'm writing these words listening to the West Clare wind battering my windows! I'm not much of a surfer but I enjoy flinging myself into the cool water, and the feeling of actually catching a wave is very special. It reminds me of when you hit a golf ball right out of the middle of the face of your driver and it feels perfect. In that moment, when the sea takes over and your board begins to accelerate with the wave, it's as if you and the ocean have momentarily signed up as partners and the water is saying, 'OK, let's see what you've got,' before it unceremoniously dumps you head first into the surf.

Lahinch is thronged with surfers, especially at the weekend, and I always enjoy watching the different kinds. There are the hardcore all-year-round guys who drive battered camper vans and organise their whole lives around the waves and tides. There are the office dreamers who tolerate their jobs in the hopes of eventually hitting the beach late some evening or at the weekends. And then there are the folks who talk about surfing. For them, it's all about strapping the thing to the roof of the car and driving up and down the promenade with no real intention of ever getting in. They check tide websites and talk loudly in work or the pub about when 'the big swell' is coming. They never seem to get any better at surfing but the quality of their gear seems to drastically improve. And when actually in the water, they sit on the board for hours, looking the part but avoiding the hard-work surfing. That's how I was approaching my meditation. If inner peace had a cool logo on a sticker, my car would have been covered in them. I was enjoying the vibes, man, without catching any gnarly tubes. OK, sorry, I'm getting carried away now. But you get what I'm saying. I had been skirting around the inner work and didn't see the big wave coming that would eventually knock me over.

When I found myself completely drained, struggling to move from the edge of the bed, I knew I had to reach out for help. The combination of unchecked stress about the comedy and radio shows and the continuous lack of sleep meant that I felt utterly wrung out. I couldn't keep going the way I was and I couldn't go it alone anymore. I brought myself to the GP's office, and before I could tell her what was bothering me, I broke down and sobbed my eyes out. I just had no fight left in me and it all came pouring out. The GP was very understanding and suggested some resources but told me what I needed more than anything at that moment was rest. I took a week off and pretty much slept the whole time.

After the week off work, I knew I had a choice. I could continue the way I was going and struggle during periods of pressure, or I could lean into the stuff I *knew* worked. One evening is particularly clear to me. I sat at my kitchen counter and opened my laptop. I searched 'meditation teacher training'. I didn't really want to be a teacher – I just wanted something that would force me to engage properly with the subject. I knew something like that would give me focus, and I felt like I was doing something really positive for myself.

The teacher I chose was a man called Davidji, who I've already mentioned. He goes by one name, like Bono or Spiderman or Shakira, and I came across him on internet radio about the time I was getting into all of this. His story caught my attention. He had spent 12 years working in the South Tower of the World Trade Centre in New York and survived the terrorist attacks but lost a lot of good friends. Afterwards, he began to question everything about his life, and a brief encounter with a homeless man changed his view forever. One day, he was walking through the backstreets of Soho in Manhattan, and as he passed some cardboard boxes where people were living, a hand shot out and grabbed his trouser leg. Looking up at him, a man said, 'What's going to be on your tombstone?' Pretty intense, right? Personally, I think falling down the stairs of a karaoke bar is classier but whatever ... He has a great book called *Sacred Powers* that tells the full story.

The one thing, though, that drew me to what he was saying was his humour. He wasn't afraid to talk about stuff like meditation and make it funny. And that really struck a chord with me. Why does the 'spiritual' community take itself so seriously? So many of the books I had read were by people who looked mildly tortured in their profile pictures. You know the ones, hands joined in prayer and held under the chin as if to say 'It's not easy being this wise but somehow I pull it off …' Sometimes, it can seem like everyone is trying to out-spiritual each other and that laughing is an unnecessary distraction from looking holy. But Davidji was funny and laughed at himself and seemed to bust all the myths I had about the world of meditation and mindfulness.

And why wouldn't we laugh? Human beings are hilarious! The way we think is unpredictable and scattered and often self-defeating. We spend ages getting it right and the next minute we fall apart. We don't know what we want and kill ourselves trying to get it. We love each other and hurt each other and put crisps in our sandwiches. We're mad as a bag of hammers! We need to laugh at ourselves because laughter is so bloody powerful. It can change everything in an instant. How often have you been rowing with a best friend or partner and, just at the moment when someone could lash out or storm off, you both break down laughing? It can take the most heated of moments and, as my mother-in-law might say, 'soften its cough' ('sicken its puke' is another one of hers but I'm still not entirely sure what it means).

And laughter is a beautiful lubricator for learning. The happier we are, the easier information goes in. Hell, they even did experiments where people put pencils in their mouths to force their face into a smile, and even that increased learning![3] If we are hoping to look under the bonnet of our thinking, which can be a testing-enough experience, it makes sense that we would make the process as enjoyable as possible. There's no reason why reinventing your thinking can't be a bit of craic!

So I signed up for Davidji's course and began reading a huge amount of texts from the scribes of ancient India to modern Buddhist philosophies. I wanted to learn more context to meditation and where it came from. I dove into the rock stars of this world, like Patanjali, Yogananda, Pema Chödrön and Shankara. (It's OK – I hadn't heard of them either.) But I wanted the science too. I wanted to find the latest studies that proved to stressed-out modern people what lads in robes knew thousands of years ago – this stuff works! The science is there and there's more emerging every day. (We'll look at a few of my favourite studies a little later on.)

One of the things I wasn't expecting in all of this work was how much it would force me to examine how I thought. We take our thinking so much for granted. In a way, it's kind of like our cars. We sit in them every day, turn the key and *vroom*! We're not examining the sound of the engine or thinking about the pistons or feeling the vibrations from the tyres on the road. Some days, we can arrive at our destination and not even really remember getting there. As part of my work, I looked at something Davidji calls your 'winning formula'. This is the way of thinking and behaving that we develop, usually between the ages of eight and fifteen, that defines how we interact with the world. Let me give you an example.

My winning formula has always been based around humour. And what an amazing resource it is. It has been my protector, my armour and weaponry, my guide for smooth passage through rough terrain. It has been a magic cloak for social occasions that were awkward, dull or unsettling. An ice-breaker, a deal-maker and the foundation for a career. And it found its roots early on.

Being the youngest of six children, it would be expected that I would never be short of company, but it doesn't always work like that. Most of my siblings were a lot older than me and left home one after the other. When we were together, family dinners were a lesson in survival of the wittiest and, as the youngest, my attempts to join in were usually met with ridicule or, at best, indifference. So I spent most of my time lost in imaginary war scenarios with my Action Man – an eagle-eyed soldier action figure who seemed to have pubes for hair. I became obsessed with tricks and pranks and would feel tremendous satisfaction when a scream from our cleaner, Mrs Hartigan, meant another fake rodent had been uncovered among the pots and pans. If people weren't going to give me attention then I was damn well going to force them, even if it took the help of a rubber rat.

I also liked Smurfs and made the fatal error of bringing some of my figurine collection to school. This was seen by one threesome of tough lads as a cardinal sin of childishness, and so began a year-long campaign of abuse and threats of 'you're dead after school'. Every day I walked the gauntlet of bigger boys on racing bikes eyeing me up, as I prayed for safe passage back to my non-judgemental Action Man. I never seemed to learn, though, and in first year of secondary school, I wore Madonna badges on my school jumper. More threats, sneers and pushes in the corridor. (I still stand by *Like a Virgin* – it's a bloody good album!) From age 10 to 15, I seemed to attract bullies – at school, on holidays, even my neighbour. On one occasion, he feigned friendship and invited me to the local disused shack on the promise of seeing a 'skin mag'. On arrival at said shack, he promptly got me in a headlock and, before punching me in the face, said, 'You should never fall for women!' Sound advice but a harshly meted-out lesson nonetheless.

I had great friends and I'm not trying to paint my childhood like it was *Lord of the Flies* but I did find myself getting picked on during those years. As my aggressors hissed and spat their threats in my face, I became mesmerised by the strength of their emotions. Why were they so angry? How had they worked themselves up into such a frenzy? And why were they in *my* face? I thought I was great! I smiled at people, said hello, was pretty much nice to everybody – I couldn't make sense of it.

One summer's day, during my school holidays, I was being held in a headlock by a local boy outside a sweet shop (bullies don't take holidays). During the tussle, I had the oddest experience. Time seemed to slow down. I remember not feeling any fear or aggression or desire to fight back. I simply felt utter curiosity about the intensity of the other boy's emotions towards me. I remember the tenseness of his arms, the smell of his clothes and the strange, angry noises he was making. But I was in an intrigued, detached state, like a scientist observing an animal's behaviour. It was a slow-motion witnessing of the interaction of two very different energetic states – mine and his. It was an experience that never left me, but as interesting as this state of witnessing was, it's not a terribly useful one when you're in the process of getting beaten up! One thing was for sure, though, my opinion of the world, and just how safe it was, changed rapidly.

Then, one day, it all stopped. I remember it vividly. I was standing in the central area of my school, a place where students gathered between classes. I was 15 years old and was approached by a boy who was set to begin hassling me for some reason. Suddenly, his friend piped up from behind, 'Leave him alone. Wheels is funny!' And there it was. The birth of my winning formula. Not only had I been declared untouchable because of my ability to make people laugh, they were also using a nickname, a sure-fire sign of acceptance.

Humour and I got on famously and I brought it every-where as time went on – to clubs, pubs, university – and, when peppered with alcohol, there was no occasion I couldn't conquer, no conversation too intimidating and no time for a Wheels that wasn't going to show the world that he was witty and entertaining. It was my badge of honour, my identity in the group and, most importantly, it worked. It defused tricky situations on film sets, got me noticed in radio and, amazingly, they started paying me for it. Then I realised I could make a living from jokes – funny equals money – and the groove in my winning formula got deeper.

And so my radio career kicked off – writer and presenter, solo and on teams. I started stand-up comedy, I got in TV commercials and guest spots on TV comedy shows. Then my own show materialised as I took over as host of *The Republic of Telly*. My winning formula even snagged me my beautiful wife when I wooed her by pretending to be a really terrible poet selling his wares in a pub.

But this is the shiny side of the winning-formula coin. The other side is not as glamorous. I was working all the time: 6 a.m. on the radio and comedy shows at night; TV in between and corporate gigs wherever space allowed. My earnings went up, but so did the stress. Alcohol was my release and adrenaline got me through most days. And you know the rest by now. A winning formula is just that, but it doesn't care for the cost, just results. It doesn't care if you're tired, burnt out, anxious, unfit or downright unhappy. It's your formula and that's how it's done.

The main point of all this is that our formula for life is designed at a very young age. It's moulded by our environment and the people in it and it sets us in motion down a particular road of behaviour. We use what skills we have to hand to navigate the situations that come our way and it puts us on a trajectory that continues for years. We don't stop to examine our behaviour because that's just, well, us. But there comes a time when all the old programming, all the old survival methods are no longer necessary or fit for purpose. And, just like we do with our smartphones, we need to update the software and install a new winning formula that reflects who we have become and not who we used to be.

Have you ever been out with a group of people and quietly wondered what you're doing there? You just don't seem to fit any more. Maybe you chose a job or a partner that reflected your needs at one point in your life but now it doesn't feel right. Perhaps you find yourself desperate to impress bosses and authority figures you don't even like. So many of us are basing our decisions on old habitual patterns of behaviour put in place 20 or 30 years ago. We were different people back then, with different circumstances, needs and expectations. To update our internal programming and move towards what's really right for us in this moment takes patience and the willingness to forgive ourselves for the choices we made. It also requires some space in our thinking to make room for the new versions of ourselves to evolve. Because when we don't listen to our minds, our bodies will let us know.

It's a very humbling thing when your body says enough is enough. We are experts at holding on, keeping it in, pushing through. Everything around us is about resilience and strength, personal bests and overcoming. There is very little in our culture about knowing when to rest, how to properly recharge our bodies and minds and when it is not just OK but *necessary* to say no. One of the best-known slogans on the planet is Nike's 'Just Do It.' Maybe they should be telling us to 'Just Do Nothing.'

Willpower and determination are powerful forces but they can only get you so far. There has to be balance beneath them or eventually the train will come off the tracks. If intellectually you get it but your actions say otherwise, then the body steps in and begins to send you signals. You become tired and your body craves rest. Strange rashes or ailments might appear; maybe headaches will develop or your weight might fluctuate. If we still don't listen, then our body will pump cortisol into our system to keep us upright. The upshot of that is broken sleep because the stress hormones are treating your body like a free gaff and are up all hours of the night. Pretty soon, you're a walking, exhausted bag of stress and that pressure has to come out. And it will come out.

Maybe you'll freak out at a cyclist, scream at the kids or unleash hell in a work meeting. Perhaps you'll cry at something stupid like a silly comment on Facebook, burst into tears while driving for no apparent reason or have a good weep on the jacks. Or maybe you'll have a strong urge to party like it's 1999. When we find it difficult to process what's happening in our minds, we can often unconsciously reach for any substance that will dislodge the stress for us. Ever had one of those friends who locks themselves in a toilet and cries for the evening? Or a mate who drinks five pints and wants to murder everyone in the chipper? This is stuff they are unable or unwilling to process while sober and the booze frees them up long enough for it to come out. There is one thing all these scenarios have in common and that's the role stress plays in our lives.

CHAPTER 7

LET'S TALK ABOUT STRESS, BABY

'm keeping this part simple for several reasons. First, I am not a doctor, a scientist or a neurologist. I studied archaeology and French and tell jokes for a living. So, for me to talk like one would be, as Oprah types like to say (you must use a Californian accent), 'not coming from an authentic place'. I could never be any of those things – not because I don't think I'm smart enough, but because I can't remember facts. I'm just not one of those people. You know the kind. You're sitting in the pub or around a dinner table and you make a passing comment about something you read or saw on the news. Suddenly, they launch into a detailed, fact-laden extravaganza of clever commentary. Statistics they read once ten years ago flow from their tongue and they remember poems from their Junior Cert like it happened yesterday. I have literally forgotten all of my degree. Four years, it took! Where's it gone? I can barely remember a meme I saw an hour ago in a WhatsApp group. My brain is designed for the gist or the feeling of something. I remember the emotions of a place, textures and smells.

I do, however, hang on to some information. I can recall the theme tunes to nearly every TV show I've ever seen, and I know vast amounts of useless information about 80s music. I can tell you who the reserve keeper for Manchester United was in 1982 (Steve Pears) but I know nothing after Sir Alex Ferguson arrived, which was when they actually began to win stuff. I know that the plastic bit on the end of your laces is called an aglet, and Starbuck's ship in *Battlestar Galactica* was a Viper Mark 1. I can recite the entire scripts to the films *Airplane!* and *Withnail and I,* and I'm actually very good at the *modh coinníollach.* This is all entirely useless for a career in academia. Unless they're showing old episodes of *Knight Rider* or playing Wham album tracks, I've no business being there.

Remembering the gist of important things will not get you hired for a TED Talk: 'And when the virus enters the … thing, it causes something … beginning with "C" to happen. This is very good, as far as I can remember, and that's why 60-ish per cent of viruses can be destroyed by a process of … I think it was something to do with lasers?' [Standing ovation.] I can read a book and a week later I've forgotten most of it. But I'll remember the photo on the front cover in great detail and what the book smelt like. And if I meet someone out of context, like if I worked with them in an old job, I'm absolutely screwed. Their name will not be available to me. But I will remember all the useless information, like the colour of their car, if they were funny or what team they supported. I confuse Carolines with Catherines and all my holidays have blended into one. So, when it comes to meditation, I'll give you the things that actually stayed with me through learning all this stuff and hopefully they'll stay with you too.

I'm also keeping this simple because, when I was hurting, I read all these self-improvement books that went into incredible detail about biology and neuroscience. It was all dehydroepiandrosterone and metacognition. I needed relief, not a PhD. I do, however, think some information on what's happening in our bodies and minds when we're stressed is helpful because being aware of it can make us feel less helpless and less bonkers. So, I might use some scientific terminology but not a lot.

So what is stress? Stress is your body's response to any threat or danger, real or imagined. It has a reputation for being a relentless danger, weaving its way into our lives and wearing us down until our bodies and minds give up. It's portrayed as something outside of us, like a mysterious black cloud that can descend at any time without warning. But here's the thing – stress has been getting a lot of negative press and it's not entirely justified. It's a bit like 'Bohemian Rhapsody' by Queen. When that tune came out, many critics hated it. Some thought it was over the top and too long. They questioned the sanity of creating a rock opera and believed many radio stations would never play it. Pretty soon, though, the song became a hit and would eventually emerge as a rock masterpiece.

The stress response of the human body is also a misjudged masterpiece. It's designed to protect us and is exceptionally good at it. It can get us out of dangerous situations and it can help get us to a level of peak performance. Stress helps us overcome obstacles and reach our goals. It pushes us to challenge ourselves and it can give us the energy to do incredible things. It causes a chain reaction of extraordinary events in our body that help us overcome all kinds of physical and mental challenges. Think of any of your favourite sports stars or performers. They all rely on the stress response to help them achieve the excellence we expect of them. It keeps them sharp and keeps them and us coming back for more. So many of us, though, live in fear of stress. When we feel our sweat pumping and our hearts beating fast, it can be alarming and disturbing. We've been conditioned to believe that stress is bad in any situation and that it will eventually be the death of us. How we perceive stress, however, could literally save our lives.

According to the American Institute of Stress, a whopping 83 per cent of American workers are experiencing work-related stress.[4] People between the ages of 30 and 49 are the most stressed group (would having children have anything to do with it, I wonder?) and women are more stressed out than men.[5] Over half say that stress from work is affecting their life at home, and 63 per cent are ready to quit their job due to stress. This sounds grim, let's be honest. But there is a statistic in all of the research that shines from the depths, like those gold coins at the end of *The Goonies*. Although 57 per cent of people surveyed said stress paralyses them, the other 43 per cent said that stress *invigorates* them. This is the key to unlocking the power of stress. What that last group of people probably aren't aware of is that their attitude to stress is literally lengthening their lives.

Here's a piece of research I'd really like you to remember. It appears in the excellent book *The Upside of Stress* by Stanford psychologist and lecturer Kelly McGonigle. University of Wisconsin researchers tracked almost 30,000 American adults for eight years.[6] As part of their study they asked participants two questions:

- Have you experienced stress in the last year?
- Do you believe that stress is harmful to your health?

They then checked public death records to see who had died and what they found was quite startling. People who had said they had experienced a lot of stress in the previous year were 43 per cent more likely to die prematurely.

Before you go running for the Xanax, just hang on because the most important bit is coming next. This was only true for people who believed that stress was harmful to their health. People who experienced a lot of stress *but didn't view stress as harmful had the lowest risk of dying.* In fact, people who had experienced stress but believed that it made them more resilient were less likely to die than people who attempted to avoid stress altogether! What this study shows us is that, not only is how we perceive stress important for our health and wellbeing, but that attempting to avoid stress doesn't get us anywhere either. We need to make friends with stress, really grow to understand it, appreciate the benefits of short, stressful challenges and ultimately make stress work for us. We will never avoid stress. In fact, our bodies were designed with stress in mind. We're set up for it. What we are not set up for, however, is stress that continues unabated for days, weeks or years on end. That is the type of chronic stress that can wear us down and burn us out. It can keep us awake at night and make us weary of the days. It can make us sick and unhappy and test us to our limits.

So we've learned that how we approach stress and how we frame our beliefs around it will determine how it affects us. Now, most importantly, we need the tools to turn off the stress response before it becomes a problem.

When I was about 17 years old, I was at a school assembly. It was Easter time and the headmaster was on stage making a draw for a prize. It was a giant chocolate Easter bunny and I hadn't even bought a ticket so I had no chance of winning. I was standing with my buddies and, like all blokes that age, taking the piss was the centre of our universe. As the draw was made, each of my friends drew back from me and began to clap and cheer wildly, as if I had won the raffle. The headmaster heard the commotion and began to beckon me to the stage. 'Mr Whelan, please come up and collect your bunny!'

I attempted to step back into the safety of the crowd, like that meme of Homer Simpson reversing into the hedge, but my friends were having far too much fun to let me escape the spotlight, so they formed an impenetrable wall and pushed me back out, shouting, 'He won, sir – Dermot has won!' By this time, the entire school of 500 students were staring at me, clapping and wondering why I wasn't collecting my fantastic prize.

'Mr Whelan! Come and get your prize!'

'I can't,' I replied. 'I – I – I didn't win. I don't have a ticket.'

'Well, what are you doing saying you won then?' he shouted into the microphone.

Now, up until this point I had blushed a lot during my life. I went pretty red at most things, especially conversations with girls or adults. But at this moment, I had reached a personal best. I could feel myself getting redder and redder, hotter and hotter. I wanted the ground to swallow me up and for the draw to be over so I could get the hell out of there. My friends, of course, were delighted with how it was all going, and if I was in their shoes and it was happening to someone else, I would have found it hilarious. But now everyone was pointing at me, not because I had won a raffle but because I was going so red! It was a self-perpetuating circle of embarrassment. My pals had never expected that it would cause my face to glow brighter than a North Korean nuke test and were staring in disbelief at my beacon of a head. It seemed to last forever until, finally, the headmaster gave up trying to coax me to the stage and wrapped up the assembly. The relief when it was over was incredible. For days after, students I didn't even know seemed delighted to remind me of just how embarrassed I'd been, with one very excited first year shouting as he passed me in the corridor, 'Look! It's the guy who turned purple!' What a claim to fame!

This story is etched in my memory for many reasons. Firstly, as traumatic as it was, it was funny as hell and is still one of those lads' stories that tends to get told on nights out. Secondly, it was a moment where my body took over and I kind of sat back as a passenger and felt my face heating up beyond anything I'd experienced before. It was like watching a science experiment unfold, except my head was the petri dish. And I also remember it because I didn't know what was making me so uncomfortable. Anyone else might have laughed it off effortlessly and things would have continued.

But something in me had triggered my stress response, and my internal alarm system was screaming out that I was under threat. Blushing and sweating were my only defence so I gave it absolute welly, until I went … well … purple. I went on to make a career out of standing in front of crowds so it's obviously something I overcame. I don't mind lots of people looking at me now but, like most, I prefer when it's on my own terms. If half of Grafton Street just turned around and pointed at me, laughing, then I would probably still turn purple!

So what was happening to me in that school assembly? I was experiencing the stress response. For you, it mightn't be triggered by a chocolate-bunny raffle. It could be meeting new people, giving a presentation, asking for a raise, driving in another country or talking about how you really feel. We're all different and sometimes we just don't know what is going to trigger our inner alarm. Often, other factors can influence how we react in a given situation. Sleep really affects my mood and my ability to cope with stressful situations. Alcohol can make us feel worried and anxious – even coffee can have a real impact on how nervous we feel in any given moment. Let's look at what happens in our bodies under stress and how meditation can help.

You've probably heard of the fight-or-flight response. It's our natural, inbuilt survival mechanism that kicks in when we perceive a threat in our environment, helping us to fight off that threat or flee the situation, i.e. run like hell. It's an unconscious process, involving almost instantaneous hormonal and physiological changes, that has saved our asses on many occasions. We need it. It literally keeps us alive. It stops us from walking into traffic or putting our hand in a lion's cage at the zoo. It's an ingenious system that is constantly monitoring our surroundings for any potential dangers, reading people's faces and body language and guiding us safely through our day. The problem arises, however, when we can't shut the process off and our body continues to overreact to non-life-threatening stressors like our jobs, relationships or finances. When your body enters the fight-or-flight response, you experience the following:

- Your heart rate increases
- Your blood pressure increases
- Your breathing becomes more rapid and shallow
- You start to perspire
- Your stress hormones surge
- Your blood sugar spikes
- Your immune system is boosted
- Your growth and sex hormones are supressed

It's quite an ingenious process when you think about it. As well as all of the above reactions, your blood moves away from your digestive organs to your arms and legs, so that you can go full Usain Bolt. Under threat, your blood will also thicken and move to your extremities so, if you get cut, you will bleed out slower. How cool is that? Under stress, your body prioritises whole systems and redistributes all kinds of chemicals and hormones to deal with different scenarios. This is why you hear of amazing feats of strength and agility carried out by people in moments of crisis. In fact, the writer Jack Kirby reportedly got the idea for the character of the Hulk after witnessing a mother lift a car off her trapped child.

This system of prioritising energy is probably familiar to any of you who are fans of science fiction. The crew of Star Trek's Starship *Enterprise* were forever diverting power from shields to life support or from transporters to hull integrity. It's as if our own systems have an internal Scotty that springs into action in intense situations, screaming, 'I know you have a presentation on quarter-three sales targets to give, Captain, but I'm giving you all the power I can!' It's an incredible system that kicks in on our behalf. But here's the thing – if we can't learn ways to shut down our emergency stress response, it starts to wear us out.

Imagine if every time you got into your car you drove it like a getaway car from a bank raid. Instead of calmly driving to your destination, you took every corner at a hundred miles an hour and pushed the revs and engine to the absolute limit. Your car wouldn't survive too long before it started to show some serious wear and tear. This is what happens if we can't find ways to calm our whole system down. If we can't interrupt the emergency mode, the systems that help us in a crisis start to work against us.

Because our Scotty has diverted power away from our body's natural health-promoting routines, over time we start to become run down and prone to illness. We can experience autoimmune conditions as our circuits try desperately to get back online. After long periods of blood moving away from our digestive organs, we lose the ability to digest our food properly and take in the nutrients we need to stay healthy. This is why we often don't look great when we're stressed out. Our normal health-promoting functions aren't working properly. So the physical toll on our bodies can be great if we allow stress to become chronic stress – stress that continues over a long period of time. Remember, we need stress to stay sharp, motivate ourselves, improve, learn and reach our goals. We just don't need it all the time.

You probably have a smoke alarm in your house. Maybe, like me, you have a dog that barks when someone comes to the door. These are very useful things. That smoke alarm can save your family's lives. It needs to function correctly and, most importantly, when we really need it. If that alarm or guard dog starts making all kinds of racket continuously, it becomes seriously annoying, wears us out and, subsequently, we lose faith in the very system we're relying on to protect us. With the relentless demands being placed on us these days, and the non-stop flood of negative news and worrying global developments, we can reach a stage where our inner alarm is constantly ringing. Emails, messages, 24-hour news cycles and notifications mean that our inner guard dog is barking away like crazy until, eventually, we are unable to distinguish between a real, significant threat and something to which we shouldn't be paying a blind bit of notice.

When our stress is allowed to go unchecked, the potential consequences can be very challenging. The effects mentioned above, such as high blood pressure, increased heart rate and raised levels of cortisol and adrenaline can lead to all kinds of health issues. For many of us, it's the emotional response that first lets us know we are struggling. You may not be consciously aware that your breathing is more shallow throughout the day or that you are perspiring more with a higher heart rate. But you might notice that you are

- anxious
- depressed
- sleeping badly
- overwhelmed
- emotional
- irritable
- impatient and reactive
- feeling isolated
- experiencing more addictive behaviour

- feeling stressed or burnt out
- experiencing brain fog

You might have all of these symptoms at once or maybe just one or two. For me, there were times when I felt that if another email arrived in my inbox, my head would explode. For many people, that sense of overwhelm is very real. It often comes with brain fog, as your brain tries desperately to sort through all the demands being put upon it. Brain fog is an extremely frustrating state, as you feel like you can't think clearly but know you have to in order to deal with everything on your plate. And even more challenging is that all of these side effects of stress can become a source of stress and anxiety in themselves. How many of us have lain in bed awake from the worry of not sleeping?

Ironically, the more things we try to remember to do when under stress, the poorer our memory becomes. Stress causes exhaustion and this impairs our attention and memory function. We can often be more stressed out because we are irritable and know that we are not treating those around us very well. It's a circular, self-fulfilling situation and it can be very hard to see a way out when you're caught in the middle of it. We can end up longing for an extended break or a dramatic change in our circumstances to free us from the cycle of stress.

A wonderful psychologist friend of mine, Adam Jensen, told me about a type of unconscious self-sabotage. This is where, in order to escape or avoid a stressful situation, we unconsciously create events or scenarios that free us from the immediate source of the stress but not in a particularly positive way. Essentially, we sort of blow things up. It might be a spontaneous affair that brings a difficult relationship to an abrupt end. Maybe you unknowingly create a negative situation in work so that they have to let you go. Or perhaps your behaviour just becomes reckless to a point where you throw all the pieces of your life in the air to see where they fall. These are all extreme options for dealing with stress, and it's never a healthy way of coping with the challenges you're facing. In an ideal scenario, if there are things in our lives that need addressing, we hope to manoeuvre through them with as much clarity, kindness and grace as possible. But if we don't have the tools to help us navigate potentially stressful situations, we can end up creating a scenario that ultimately gets us what we want but not in a way that would make us particularly proud when we look back on it.

I knew a person who was very good in their chosen field. They had all the talents required to do a difficult job, and they were generally a happy, upbeat person. After a while, however, demands of the job started to wear them down. They began to show all the signs of stress. They were moody and irritable and their attitude became snarky, defensive and sarcastic. People were less inclined to deal with them because of their difficult demeanour and so they began to be avoided and overlooked for important meetings and events. A few close colleagues had a chat with them and pointed out what was happening, encouraging them to seek help for the stress they were experiencing. Little changed, however, and they doubled down on the resistance, often saying and doing things that were sure to aggravate those in charge. Eventually it came to a head and, at the first opportunity for structural change in the company, they were let go. What was sad was that they really loved their job and didn't want to leave. But their reaction to the stress they were under, for whatever reasons, meant they began unconsciously to create a situation that made it difficult for management to keep them on.

Months later, I met them on the street and they were much happier. They had found new employment and were excited to be doing something new. But they regretted how their previous job had ended and felt that their bridges had been burnt to some extent. They were confused about how pear-shaped it had gone and were saddened by the nature of their exit. It felt like unfinished business to them and they were left wondering what might have been.

This is the thing with unchecked stress. It can turn us into versions of ourselves that we don't really like. And we all react differently. Some of us become prickly and defiant and are prone to lashing out. Others become negative, cynical and sarcastic. Many deal with ongoing stress by retreating into themselves and become isolated and withdrawn. And others escape into addictive behaviour that temporarily numbs the discomfort. Most of us will experience all of the above at some point because dealing with the stresses of our modern lives can be tough if we don't have any of the skills that can give us relief. Places where we usually thrive can feel threatening or difficult. Maybe we manage to keep our head above water in work but bring the stress home to the people we love. Perhaps you're confused and disappointed about why you're so touchy at home. Sometimes, we can lose touch with the people we used to be and wonder if we'll ever get back to our old selves. And the answer is yes, of course we can. It just takes a bit of awareness, knowledge and practice and pretty soon we're singing in the shower again, but that's a story for later on.

So where does meditation come in? Well, meditation allows us to turn off that stress response. It is the 'pattern interrupt' to the flow of overwhelming information coming our way every day, and it can help to reverse all the effects of stress mentioned above. Meditation has been scientifically proven to counteract stress in these ways:

- reduces heart rate
- lowers blood pressure
- reduces stress hormones
- boosts the immune system
- regulates perspiration

- improves sleep
- aids digestion
- balances emotions
- decreases anxiety and depression
- relaxes breathing
- lessens overwhelm
- reduces brain fog
- boosts creativity
- helps us to make better decisions
- improves our sense of happiness and fulfilment

If a plant down in Ringaskiddy was making a pill that would do all the above, we'd all have shares in the place. But I'm convinced that because meditation is free and open to everyone, we tend to undervalue or overlook it. It seems almost too easy. You can be sure that if those pharmaceutical companies could patent it and charge for it they would! Thankfully, it's as free as the air and all the science, especially over the last ten years, points to real, tangible results in making us happier, less anxious, more fulfilled versions of ourselves.

Let's look at some of the scientific studies that show the impact of chronic stress on our bodies and minds and what meditation can do to relieve the effects. These are the ones that really caught my eye and helped get me into this stuff. First up, shrinking amygdalas. In 2011, 16 people took part in a Harvard-affiliated study at Massachusetts General

Hospital.[7] Each person meditated on average for 27 minutes per day for a period of 56 days, or 8 weeks. They were not regular meditators, possibly like many of you reading this book right now. In addition to weekly mindfulness sessions, in which they practised awareness of sensations and feelings, they also listened to guided meditations. Before, during and after the study, their brains were examined using MRI (Magnetic Resonance Imaging), as were the brains of a control group who did not take part in the meditation practice. The results were startling. After the 56-day period, the research showed actual physical changes in the brains of the participants. Most notably, the part of the brain responsible for processing emotions, particularly fear, the amygdala, *had shrunk in size.* There was less actual grey matter in that part of the brain. Conversely, the part of the brain that is important for memory and learning, as well as compassion and self-awareness, actually increased in density. There was more of it!

This was a light-bulb moment for me. It became really clear. How can we continue to have the same amount of fearful, anxious or angry thoughts if the part of our brain that is responsible for them is shrinking? It is, if you'll excuse the pun, a no-brainer. Up until this point, the brains of regular meditators had, in studies, shown structural differences to those of non-meditators, but it couldn't be proven if meditation was the cause. Now, however, the science showed that the reported benefits of meditation were not just down to people having nice relaxing periods on a cushion with their eyes closed.

'Although the practice of meditation is associated with a sense of peacefulness and physical relaxation, practitioners have long claimed that meditation also provides cognitive and psychological benefits that persist throughout the day,' says study senior author Sara Lazar of the MGH Psychiatric Neuroimaging Research Program and a Harvard Medical School instructor in psychology. 'This study demonstrates that changes in brain structure may underlie some of these reported improvements and that people are not just feeling better because they are spending time relaxing.'

This was huge for me to learn early on because, I suppose, I always had some doubts about whether meditation was a credible tool for brain health and not just a fluffy pastime that made you sound woke. Best of all, these weren't Shaolin monks who balanced on one leg for eight hours a day in a closed monastery all their lives. These were people like you and me who were new to all of this. If I could change the physical structure of my brain in less than two months, then it begged the question: what else could I change?

For many people, just the thought of sitting down to meditate can fill them with dread. I see some people at my corporate events who can't sit still. They literally find it impossible to stay in the chair for any length of time.

Sometimes they suffer through; sometimes they get up and leave. I always feel proud of them for getting themselves there in the first place. It can't have been easy, and I'm sure they are often disappointed that they couldn't stick it out. But turning up is always a win, and the next time might be the time when something clicks. Sitting with ourselves sounds so easy, doesn't it? Until we try. Then we realise how many demands there are on our attention every minute of every day. Our minds are like puppies that have had chew toys dangled in front of them for years, only for them to be taken away in an instant when we sit down. The poor puppies don't know what to do so they start chasing their tails.

Lots of people come to me feeling as if their brains are like a glitchy iPhone. They say things like, 'There's something wrong with me, I have too many thoughts,' or 'Other people can do this but my brain just isn't wired for meditation.' One woman told me that she hated spending time with herself because she was too boring! If you find the idea of sitting in silence with your thoughts a bit daunting, don't worry. Science proves that you are not alone. In fact, it proves that most of us would rather inflict pain on ourselves than sit alone in a room for fifteen minutes.

This is one of my favourite studies. The University of Virginia in Charlottesville, USA, carried out a study into people's attitudes to being left alone with their thoughts.[8]

They gathered together hundreds of undergraduates and members of the community, of all ages, and set them a task. They had to sit in a sparsely furnished room by themselves, with no obvious distractions, for periods of between six and fifteen minutes. They did not have access to their phones or other devices for the duration. There was, however, another feature of the experiment. On the table in front of them was a button. When pressed, this button would administer an electric shock to the test participant. They had the option of pressing the button if they wanted. Otherwise, they could choose to ignore it and, in doing so, avoid experiencing any unnecessary pain.

The results were literally shocking – 67 per cent of the men involved in the test and 25 per cent of the women chose to press the button and electrocute themselves. Some of them multiple times. In fact, one male participant electrocuted himself a total of 190 times in one 15-minute period! What is wrong with us? Are we really that uncomfortable with being alone with our own minds that we would rather inflict actual pain on ourselves than expose ourselves to silence for a few minutes? It's also worth noting that, in advance of the experiment, each person who pressed the button had already had a chance to try out the device to see how painful it was. All of them had said they would pay money not to experience it again. But they all did – willingly! The man behind the experiment, Timothy Wilson, admitted, 'I'm puzzled by that.'[9]

As humans, we're so good at interacting with our surroundings. We love to engage our minds, driven by curiosity, desires and survival. So when we sit still and go inward, it can seem unnatural. Primal instincts might make us feel vulnerable because we're not watching our backs, or we could experience pangs of FOMO as we wonder what else is going on in our phones or on the telly. But when we meditate, we gradually learn that it's OK to unplug from the interactive matrix for a while. We can pull that Neo-style plug out of the back of our neck and give ourselves a chance to refresh. We do it with our computers and devices all the time. We close down tabs we don't need, we close apps that drain our batteries, we reboot our laptops when they're sluggish. Why not do it to ourselves? It's easy, it's quick and it's painless. Unless, of course, you'd rather run a few hundred volts through your body …

The next experiment I want to bring to you reminds me of a classic quote from Homer Simpson. It's from the episode where he volunteers as a marriage counsellor at the local community centre: 'To the untrained eye, I'm eating an orange. But to the eye that has brains, I'm making a point about marriage. For you see, marriage is a lot like an orange. First, you have the skin. Then the sweet, sweet innards.'

Mmmm. Innards … I think it's fair to say that, when our closest relationships are operating well, we tend to be happier and less stressed. When it comes to our other halves, we all want things to be running smoothly. Happy wife, happy life and all that ... What's that? Your relationship is perfect and you don't need any help whatsoever? Respect! But for the other 99.9 per cent of you who wouldn't mind a helpful hint in the that department, we'll have a look at a study that was carried out in in 2004 in the University of North Carolina.[10]

For this study, the research focused on what they referred to as 'relatively happy, non-distressed couples'. Sure, what more could we hope for in a relationship? Basically, the couples involved weren't at each other's throats 24 hours a day and had to have been together for at least 12 months. Given that they were already pretty content together, any improvement in the relationship would be quite significant. Half of the group were given an eight-week mindfulness training programme and then were compared to the half that did not receive the treatment until later. Among the things they were taught were exercises to bring them into the present moment and how to direct positive feelings towards their loved ones. The results were pretty remarkable. They all ended up divorced. Only kidding.

All couples experienced a boost in satisfaction levels with their relationships by as much as 50 per cent. They also experienced a drop in interpersonal stress and related problems by as much as 50 per cent. Basically, they were way happier together, even though they were pretty happy to begin with. Most couples were really happy about the mindfulness aspect of the experience. 'We've shifted out of the "automatic mode" we were stuck in,' said one couple who had been together for twenty years. 'We're kinder, more accepting and understanding of one another now, more at ease even when we're at our worst. And on good days, we relate much better than we ever did before.' Who wouldn't want a bit of that action?

Another couple reported being more aware of how valuable each moment was and found that it was not worth ruining the present by dwelling on past difficulties. And one woman said she and her husband experienced more togetherness following the study, instead of being like roommates who shared the same house. Then there was the 'strawberry woman' who, frankly, terrifies me. After her husband dropped a bowl of chocolate-covered strawberries (la-di-da), she admitted to having thoughts like, 'He intentionally did this, he always does this kind of thing!' Harsh. 'But,' she says, 'I was surprised to find that, at the same time, I was very clearly noticing exactly what I was going through. I noticed the tension in my stomach and face, the heat in my body, the change in my breathing, the feelings of hurt and irritation and exactly what thoughts I was having.' Eh, it's a bowl of bleedin' strawberries …

'I saw that I had a strong urge to strike out at him in some way, to say something mean and cutting, but that's not what I did. I recognised in that moment that I had a choice to not react automatically. As I stood there, I noticed the apprehension on my husband's face, and my thoughts changed to "It was an accident, we all make accidents. I can be gentle if I want."

'I walked over and gave him a big hug. He was very surprised, and so was I! He apologised, and I asked him to please be more careful, more mindful. After this, I felt elated and a sense of freedom. And instead of spending several hours punishing him, I was able to enjoy being with him. I said to myself, "Mindfulness is really working!"' I can't help but feel sorry for that guy. Let's hope she keeps it up! Otherwise, he may be found lifeless and face down in a Wexford punnet.

Strawberry murders dipped in chocolate aside, meditation really works in a relationship. My wife and I have definitely benefited from it. We laugh more at stuff that may have irritated us before. We're more patient with each other and the children, and we empathise a lot more with each other. We can appreciate what it's like to be in each other's shoes (sadly, her heels don't suit me). And that's not surprising. Science shows that meditation boosts the part of our brain responsible for empathy.[11] The temporo-parietal junction may sound like something you would hear in an AA Roadwatch traffic report, but it's the part of the brain that, when activated, allows us to appreciate where someone else is coming from. Meditation, when practised regularly, strengthens this area of our grey matter. You could say it actually makes us kinder, nicer, more understanding people. Unless you're dropping chocolate-covered strawberries everywhere. Then it's every man for himself!

So, science proves that meditation makes you more self-aware, boosts memory, improves your relationships, makes you kinder to yourself and others, helps you sleep better and every other benefit we discussed at the start of this chapter. But most meditators aren't focusing on the science when they practise. They're not jumping up from their cushions shouting, 'Hooray! I shrank my amygdala!' They're just enjoying it. If you've ever played sport or worked out regularly, you know that if you stop doing it can be like something is missing. It's the same with meditation. Sometimes, it's only when we're not doing it any more that we realise just how good it was making us feel.

CHAPTER 8

WHAT MEDITATION IS ... AND ISN'T

S*he awoke at the same time she always did: 5.05 a.m. She didn't even need an alarm any more. Her smooth tanned feet felt the coolness of the floorboards. The bashful sun had yet to reach the fullness of its heat and the dawn chill still hung in the air. The white linen glided over her skin and she revelled in the looseness of the fabric. She seemed to float down the stairs, past the photos that reminded her of who she had become: base camp at Everest with her guide, the joyful bead ceremony at an Indian retreat, the embrace with her precious guru. In all, she smiled with a new-found intensity, a smile that shone from within rather than from her face. Her hand gently touched the latch and the glass door slid back to invite in a day like no other.*

The garden was still but for the small birds already bobbing to and fro on the manicured lawn. The acacia trees stood tall, their long branches hanging low over the old walls, heavy with flowers. She crossed the paving stones and headed for the small wooden gate at the end of the garden. Barefoot, she enjoyed the grounding sensation from the stone and grass as she followed the winding path through the greenery. The jetty glistened with the last of the fading dew, and beyond that lay the lake. The calm surface stretched out in front of her like morning's mirror, and soon she found herself at the end of the wooden walkway.

She breathed in the full lake air and, placing her small woollen mat beneath her, sat into her familiar lotus position. She closed her eyes and allowed her surroundings to guide her to her centre. This is where she had come to meditate at the beginning of every day for the past year, since she had left behind the trappings of the hectic financial world. A new version of her innermost self was emerging. Her breath found a slow rhythm and she felt herself settle in, calm and peaceful but alert to the complexity of the natural beauty around her. Once again, she was everywhere and nowhere. More than that, she was home ...

And this, my friends, is a load of bollox. It is not real. But, for some reason, if you put 'meditation' into Google, you'll be bombarded by images of beautiful women in white linen perched on jetties. Seriously, why all the wooden jetties? I've only ever walked down one wooden jetty and it was really wet and slippy and green from some kind of slithery moss. It was in Ireland, so naturally it was cold and windy, and the only thing I would get from sitting down to meditate on it would be a damp arse and hypothermia. And white linen just does not work on Irish people. We either look like we're in our pyjamas or are psychiatric patients and, as my mother might say, there's no heat in it. But this is one of the classic images that seems to follow meditation around.

Another favourite is the mountaintop. Usually, it's men we see up there, sitting on a rocky outcrop, ready for enlightenment. I don't know about you, but if I sit on rocks for any length of time I get a numb backside or a dead leg. A mountaintop can, I admit, be an impressive spot on which to hang out and meditate, but it's a huge amount of work getting there. Scaling K2 every morning before breakfast just feels like too much effort. I think I'd prefer my favourite chair.

And then, of course, there are the images of people meditating on a perfect beach at sunrise or sunset. It's like the makers of every Bounty bar advert from the 1970s until now have posted endless photos of flawless humans on flawless sand, fingers and thumbs joined, with their legs tied up like a Bavarian pretzel. It's all so wonderfully Instagram. And all these clichéd images of people in a classic meditation pose throw up one very important question – *who's taking the photo?* It's hard to find enlightenment when your best mate is standing behind you with an iPhone. There isn't really a filter for inner peace, and meditation is supposed to be an inward adventure to the calmer, reflective, less judgemental parts of you, not an outward one to the reactive, frantic, judge-y world of the internet. If you're more worried about how flowy your silk yoga pants look by the lakeside than quietening your mind, then you are going to struggle with the whole process. So ignore the imagery you see online – including, by the way, those little stacks of flat stones that seem to crop up everywhere for some reason ...

Meditation is also not a cult or a religion. You will not have to move to a ranch in Arkansas or walk around Grafton Street banging a drum. There is no great leader who will lead you to the spaceship, and you do not need to barely wear underpants and live in a cave. Caves have terrible BER ratings anyway. Yes, meditation came from Eastern philosophies and religions, which had their own customs, traditions and dodgy outfits, but it is a tool for everyone, from every era and background, and you can also wear trousers if that's your thing.

You may or may not want to dip into the more ancient texts and sources. It depends on what floats your boat. Perhaps, like me, you'll start off simply and, over time, find yourself drawn to learn more. The ancient Indian philosophical text the *Bhagavad Gita* is one that I enjoy reading and, apparently, has heavily influenced actor and musician Will Smith. So if it's good enough for the Fresh Prince then it must have something going for it. If you are already religious, meditation will not conflict with that and, in fact, should be a nice complement to your faith, whatever that may be.

And if you want to treat it the same way you treat your daily physical exercise routine – just something you do to make yourself feel better – then that's perfect too.

Debunking these myths around meditation is actually one of the things that led me to become a teacher. As I mentioned earlier, I initially just wanted to do the teacher training so that I would lean into the things that I knew helped me better deal with stress. But the more I learned about meditation, the simpler it became. All the books I read, all the time I spent examining my own behaviour seemed to be pointing to the same thing. The simplicity of meditation is the key.

There is a line in chapter 2, verse 48 of the *Bhagavad Gita*: *'Yogasthah kuru karmani.'* Maybe you didn't learn the ancient Sanskrit language for the Junior Cert, so I'll translate it. In essence, it means 'establish yourself in the present moment and then perform action'. This is all we really need to do. When we can cultivate the awareness to spend as much of our time in the present moment, everything gets easier. When we spend less time in the past, worrying about what happened, and less time in the future, worrying about what might happen, then we can get on with the business of being our genuine, happy selves.

This is the simple message that made me want to become a teacher. I realised that if I could use my comedic skills and all my media experience to help people stay in the here and now just a little bit more, I would really be making a difference. I was living proof that this stuff works. I went to a teacher-training course in California, and as soon as I returned, I began to teach. I was nervous at first because I was afraid how people might perceive me outside of my comedian role. So I started small, with groups of colleagues and close friends, until I found a bit more confidence in the space. Any time I began to have doubts, I reminded myself that this was not about me. It was about using my talents and experience to help others reconnect with themselves. In my head I coined the phrase, 'I can't be nervous if I'm in service.' It seemed to do the trick and I still use it if ever my ego is getting in the way.

In my introduction, I mentioned that special day when 30 insurance workers seemed more dazzling than thousands at the 3Arena. And that has continued to be my path. Since 2019 I've been working with some of the biggest companies in the world, sharing simple techniques to navigate stress and stay in the present moment. I've given talks to scientists in Northern Italy and to sales teams at Google. The nature of the business doesn't matter because they all have the same thing at their core – people. I've shared the same methods you're about to learn with schools and cancer support groups. Whatever our path in life, we all want the same things – less stress and more fulfilment.

So what exactly *is* meditation? Here is my simplest definition. Meditation is focusing your mind on one thing. And when your mind wanders off, which it will, you gently bring your attention back to the thing you were focusing on. That's it. Put down the book. We're done.

Bye for now,

Dermot.

OK, we'll talk some more about it. But that's really all there is to it. People are often shocked or dismayed at this explanation of meditation because they expected more. Sometimes, they're disappointed because they were hoping for layers and levels and secret passwords. But that stuff is often unnecessary and is sometimes just a ruse to get you to part with your money. We sit, we focus, and when our mind wanders, we gently guide it back. *Sin é*, as the man says. Another myth is that, in meditation, we are attempting to clear our mind of all thoughts. That's like trying to clear children out of a birthday party as the cake arrives. It's just not going to happen. We have between 60,000 and 80,000 thoughts per day, so trying to eliminate them altogether seems like an insurmountable task.

Think of them like wasps on your pint in a beer garden. They just keep coming. And trying to swipe them away is futile. They're relentless. So we decide to live with them. And maybe, after a while, we'll become more tolerant, perhaps even begin to look a bit closer at them and appreciate their busyness and resilience. They're just doing what they've been programmed to do. I think I've stretched this analogy as far as it can go. And I appreciate that a lot of you just hate wasps, end of story. But you get what I'm saying? We need thoughts – without them we would be dead. They are a sign that we are alive and functioning as human beings, but trying to make them go away is exhausting. So we learn to sit with them until we make peace with them and appreciate that they are just trying to do their job. Thoughts, in themselves, are harmless, but if we give them too much power (OK, one more wasp comparison), we get stung. So meditation gives us the space to witness our thoughts as they go about their business and, over time, we begin to spend more time with thoughts that are a better match for how we want to feel.

One day I was sitting with my friend Peter in a pub in Galway. We were waiting for our food to arrive and he was on Tinder. He's a good bit younger than me. He swiped through his phone, scanning the faces and profiles that popped up. Being from a generation where dating meant cycling past someone's house until they noticed you, I had never used Tinder, and I was fascinated by the thought pro-cess in choosing a match.

One thing struck me more than anything else – he was so fussy! Peter was swiping left on almost everybody he saw, for the most random reasons. And I've found the same thing with other Tinder users, men and women. Not that I follow single people around and sit next to them rubbing my legs while they use Tinder. But it's primarily left, left, left. And there is nothing wrong with having high standards and not just saying yes to anyone with a head. But it got me thinking. We are so choosy when it comes to finding a date. So why aren't we as fussy when it comes to the thoughts with which we spend our time?

These thoughts are literally filling our heads and our days. We blindly swipe right on negative or unhelpful ones, wining and dining them, even though they have the power to make us miserable. Sometimes they stick around for the long haul. And there's a name for a thought that we keep on having: a belief. And beliefs can be lifelong companions. 'I'm worthless.' 'I'm a mess.' 'I'm not enough.' 'I'm ugly.' We can be swiping right on all these thoughts for years before we realise what's happening and, for many of us, we never even know we're married to them. We have a choice in every moment of how we want to feel, and the thoughts on which we swipe right have to be the right ones.

Meditation is Tinder for your thoughts. It makes you aware of those you're spending most time with and gives you a choice as to whether you wish to continue. All it takes is a regular meditation routine and pretty soon you'll know exactly what kind of thoughts you're shacked up with on a daily basis. With up to 80,000 per day, you can't control each one. But you can get a grip on the kinds of things that fill your head and ask yourself which are the thoughts you would like to date – the ones that make you feel confident, happy and calm, or the ones that hide fish behind your radiator, wee in your kettle and rob all your toilet roll?

CHAPTER 9

THIS IS HOW WE DO IT

Yes, that is a Montell Jordan reference. Deal with it. This is how we do it. The meditation, that is. We're going to do some techniques that really helped me. For the purpose of explaining the meditations, I have written them out for you in this section. You will also find the recorded audio version of each of them on my website. These are free and exclusive to all my fantabulous readers. Just go to www.dermotwhelan.com and enter the code MINDFULL21. They have different benefits and effects and I really recommend you try them at the time of reading so you get a feel for them. My purpose here is to give you a taste of the different kinds of meditation available. I'm not expecting you to love them all, so don't worry if one or two aren't doing much for you. Meditation is a bit like listening to music: some styles resonate with you and some don't. It's about flicking through the albums to see what fits.

So let's remind ourselves what meditation is. Meditation is focusing your mind on one thing – say, for instance, your breath – and when your mind wanders, which it will, we gently guide it back to the focus of our attention. I say 'gently' because meditation is not supposed to be another reason to beat ourselves up. One of the reasons we are sitting down to close our eyes is to move away from being so hard on ourselves all the time. So if we use our meditation time to give out to ourselves internally, we're kind of defeating the purpose. This is self-care, not self-criticism, so let's be kind with those thoughts and tell the nun on the end of the bed to go watch *Sister Act* for a while (but not *Sister Act 2: Back in the Habit* because that's really terrible). You're reading this book because a part of you is sick and tired of berating yourself for thinking or acting certain ways, so welcome a new exercise like meditation that is a self-criticism-free zone. My God, that's a lot of hyphens. Remember, you have exclusive access to my guided meditations and you can take those one step at a time. In the meantime, though, let's look at the different styles of meditation that you might come across.

GUIDED MEDITATIONS

These are a great place to start. A guided meditation is where you simply listen to an audio recording and follow the teacher's instructions. A lot of beginners like to start here. It's just like sliding into the passenger seat and letting someone else take over the driving for a while. Sometimes, when we feel overwhelmed, it can be a great relief just to put in headphones, hit play and let a soothing voice direct you towards a place of calm.

I relied on these so much when I was struggling. Before many stand-up shows, I could be found on my hotel bed, with the room in near darkness, drifting off to guided meditations that were the only thing that could calm down my body and mind. After a while, they became like a familiar blanket or an old reliable friend, something I could surround myself with that could raise my mood and comfort my brain. That's what happens when we find ones that resonate with us. We almost wear a groove in them from listening so often. We know the words so well we could repeat them off by heart if we had to.

But finding a guided meditation that really works for you is a bit like trying on shoes. You have to listen to lots of types to find ones that fit, that feel comfy and that suit you. If there's anything in the meditation that annoys you, it just won't work for you. It's a very intimate experience. You're literally inviting the teacher right into your head! You're sharing your innermost thoughts with this person so they have to be a good match. As you lie in the intimacy of your bed with the headphones in, you have to feel comfortable with the voice that's taking you on the journey.

One of the first things that caught my attention about my teacher, Davidji, was his voice. He was born in New

York but lives in California so has a great mix of accents. His tone is deep and smooth and he seems to use your skull as an acoustic amplifier. The first time I had him on my radio show, a listener described his voice as 'the first sip of a pint of Guinness'. Is there any greater Irish compliment you could give to someone?

Now, after years of listening to his meditations, his voice has become a kind of subconscious cue, which means the minute I hear his voice everything starts to relax. Like a lullaby to a baby, it just brings me into a calmer state. It's basically the opposite of when I hear the theme tune to *Eastenders*. That makes me sweaty and anxious – that Walford crowd are so angry and miserable! I listen to other teachers too, of course, but Davidji is definitely my favourite, and I find myself gravitating back towards him all the time. The fact that he's a very special friend of mine adds an extra dimension to his meditations as well. You will probably find that too – that you'll have one or two favourites you keep revisiting, who seem to calm you better than anyone else. So it's important to try out as many different teachers as you can.

Accents can play a large role in whether a teacher resonates with you or not. Personally, I like most American accents but you may not. Sometimes, people like to listen to accents from their own country. Or maybe it's a regional UK or an Australian voice you need to relax your nervous system. On Apple's Calm app, there's a deep-voiced French man who is extremely popular. He makes every bedtime tale sound like a sexy French film – 'You aaare feel-eeng verah relaaaxed-aaahh … ' Whatever works for you! You may also find that you have a preference for a male or a female voice. I like both.

Teachers styles differ too. Some are soft and floaty; others are more instructional and to the point. Some teachers like to talk the whole way through the meditation; others like to leave more space for you to direct your own thoughts. Some have music; some meditations are just the voice alone.

The length can also vary from a minute or two to meditations of an hour or more. There are many to choose from and lots of places you can find them. YouTube is full of guided meditations, as are the many apps out there – a few of my favourites are Insight Timer, Headspace and Unplug. Some are free; some are behind a pay wall. How much you're willing to pay is up to you. My guided meditations are free but I can't guarantee that my voice is the first sip of a pint of Guinness – it may be just the second or third.

BREATHING MEDITATIONS

These pretty much do what it says on the tin, as that advert used to say. We bring our attention to our breath and become aware of it. I'm using terms like 'bring our attention' and 'become aware of it' because that's as much effort as we make. It's not a case of focusing or concentrating so hard that your brow is furrowed, your face is getting red and

you're straining under the pressure. It's a detached observation, like you're people-watching from a café. Actually,
maybe not that, because we tend to judge people when we're
watching them and we're supposed to be non-judgemental
here. How about we do it like you're watching your children
play in the garden? Actually, no, if your children are like
mine then they're probably sliding down the slide backwards
on top of each other and you're worried they're going to
break their necks. Let's try detached observation, like you're
looking at the waves from the beach, like those weird old
couples that spend hours driving to the seaside but never
actually get out of the car. We can't control the ocean: we
simply sit and watch our breaths drift in and out.

The breath is very powerful for relaxing your nervous
system and it's amazing how we can go through most of our
lives without ever really thinking about it. Once we bring
our attention to our breath, though, we can really tap into
that present moment we hear so much about these days.
This is where we want to be because if we're in the future in
our thoughts and mind, we're worrying about what might
happen. If we're stuck in the past, we're regretting what
did happen. The present moment is the sweet spot between
the two, and that's where we give our bodies and minds a
chance to connect with each other and relax the cacks, so
to speak. In a breathing meditation, we focus our attention
on the breath, and we simply watch the breath go in and

then follow the path of the breath back out. Simple as that. Meditations can take as long as you like. You can do short ones or sit for longer periods. But before we can get started, we need to learn how to breathe.

Believe it or not, breathing is a skill. It's one we're all born with and our bodies know exactly how to do it. If you watch a newborn baby, it will breathe in a wonderfully relaxed manner. Its belly and chest will rise and fall with each breath as it gives in to our innate ability to take what we need from the air around us. The breaths will be deep, slow and mostly through the nose. Somewhere along the way, though, we decided breathing properly was just too much hassle and, instead, we became a nation of slack-jawed mouth-breathers, only closing our gobs to stop the drool splashing off the kitchen tiles. Actually, mouth-breathing is due to many factors, including our diet, which has changed considerably over the last couple of hundred years. More soft foods means our jaws aren't as developed as they used to be and this has affected how we breathe. As well as this, most of us spend our days breathing in a shallow manner into the top of our chest. It's a habit we all fall into at some stage. Instead of using our diaphragms and the supporting muscles to breathe, we use our shoulders, neck and chest, and this can lead to headaches, tension and fatigue.

There are many reasons why we fall into the habit of shallow breathing – poor posture at work, blocked sinuses, wonky noses or an unexplainable desire to catch flies in our mouths. Would you believe, one of the biggest reasons we end up with irregular or restricted breathing patterns is social pressure to have a flat tummy. It's all about the washboard abs these days and, because we don't want people to see our puppy fat, we hold in our bellies, and soon we're breathing into only the top of our lungs or barely breathing at all!

We need to think about relearning to breathe properly for a few reasons. (By the way, I bet you're focusing on how you breathe while you read this. It's OK – I'm doing it as I write!) Firstly, when our breathing is shallow, we are not pulling air into the lower part of our lungs. In this part of the lungs, there are lots of blood vessels designed to carry oxygen to all our cells. If we're constantly breathing into just the top of our lungs, we don't get the necessary oxygen to keep us energised and healthy.

Secondly, how we breathe can also affect how we think. In fact, a recent study from Northwestern University in Illinois shows a direct link between nasal breathing and enhanced memory function in the brain.[12] The experiments in this piece of research centred around monitoring people's cognitive skills during different breathing patterns. The study showed that participants were better able to remember objects and identify fearful faces when breathing in through their noses. So how they breathed had a direct influence on their memory function and their ability to react to a potential threat. When they breathed through the mouth, however, the enhanced abilities disappeared. Another black mark for mouth-breathing.

Thirdly, shallow breathing into our chests can also trigger our stress response and leave us feeling wired and anxious. It stimulates our sympathetic nervous system, which prepares us for an impending threat. It increases our heart rate, pumps our blood pressure and gets us ready for flight or flight. Thankfully, simple breathing techniques can bring our systems back online, kickstarting our parasympathetic nervous system, which calms everything down and reintroduces a much needed sense of calm. When I hear the term parasympathetic, I always think of a parachute, smoothly gliding us back down to our more grounded selves.

So let's do a simple exercise that can relax us in just a few seconds and encourage better, more effective breathing.

BELLY BREATHING

Lie down on the floor or on your bed. Alternatively, you can do this sitting in a chair with your knees bent and your head and shoulders nice and relaxed.

Place one leg behind your head and clap your hands repeatedly. Only kidding. Put one hand on your belly, just below your rib cage, and one on your chest.

Take a nice long, slow, deep breath in through your nose. Feel the air go down towards your belly. The hand on your chest should stay still but the one on your belly should rise with the breath.

Hold the breath in your belly for a moment or two and then release the breath through your mouth with your lips pursed like you're trying to blow through a keyhole, something which would really freak out your neighbours.

Try and make the exhalation last for as long as is comfortable. As you breathe out, you should feel your belly under your hand fall back towards the floor.

Repeat a few times until your boss tells you to get off the floor and back to work.

'I'd like to meditate but I just don't have the time'
– Everybody in the world

We are busy people. We have a lot on our plate. Sometimes we have lots of plates. Life can be a constant attempt to keep them all spinning, under the constant threat that they might just all fall. So many of our days are mapped out in advance, from the minute we open our eyes to when we fall into bed, saying things like, 'What a day!' Then we rinse and repeat for the rest of the week. Adding something new into an already hectic schedule of work, kids, NCTs, meetings, drinks, exercise, pick-ups and drop-offs can seem too much. And if meditation required you to sit in the lotus position for an hour every morning to begin with, it *would* be too much. Working on relaxing our nervous systems and freeing up our brains is all very well, but it can't take up all our time or we'd never get anything done. And we certainly won't keep up the meditation practice if we feel it's putting us under too much pressure. Allow me to present the 16-second meditation!

It literally takes 16 seconds of your day and busts the hell out of any 'I don't have the time' excuses. You could literally spend 16 seconds trying to open a packet of rashers. (I really can't cope with those 'Peel Here' flaps that will ABSOLUTELY NEVER PEEL! You just spend ages picking away at the plastic feeling like an idiot. And if you've got wet hands, forget it! I mean, do they never test them? Ahem, I need to meditate …) This was the first meditation that I learned and it really got me hooked. It's so simple and was passed on by my teacher, Davidji. You can read more about it in his amazing book *Secrets of Meditation*. Sometimes it's called box breathing or square breathing.

Basically, it's a counting meditation, meaning you count silently as you breathe. The idea is that you breathe in to a count of four, hold that breath in for a count of four, release the breath to a count of four and, finally, hold the breath out for a count of four. That's your 16 seconds. Pretty simple, isn't it? You may be wondering how something so short could be any help, but it is extremely effective, and I get messages from many people telling me what an enormous difference this little meditation has made for them. All the wonderful benefits we've mentioned above are taking place when you practise this technique, even in the short space of time it takes. Your heart rate will drop, your blood pressure will lower, your stress hormones will reduce and you'll begin to find a bit of stillness and silence in your day. It's the meditation equivalent of Peter Stringer – small, reliable and gets the job done!

To feel its effectiveness, let's just do an inventory of how how we feel right now. Imagine you're a pilot checking all your instruments before take-off. Close your eyes for a moment and see how you feel in your body – actually, open them again because you can't read this otherwise. Scan your body and mind. Do you feel any discomfort anywhere? Any stiffness in your neck and shoulders? How restful is your mind? See if you can give yourself a stress score out of ten – ten being as stressed as Ryan Tubridy on the *Late Late Toy Show* when the toys won't work and zero being as relaxed and content as Ryan Tubridy the day *after* the *Late Late Toy Show*. Give yourself a number, keep an open mind and let's begin.

16-SECOND MEDITATION

Take a nice long, slow, deep breath in through your nose. Feel your belly rise with your inhale. Hold the breath in your belly for a moment. Let the breath go, throught the nose or mouth, following its path as it travels up through your body and back out into the room.

Let's do one more of those. Sure it'd be rude not to, says he. Take a nice, long, slow, deep breath in through the nose. Feel the belly rise. Hold the breath for a second or two and gently let it go, following the breath back out, feeling the belly move back down.

Well done. Now we're going to try the 16-second meditation. Take a nice, long, slow, deep breath in to the count of four. One ... two ... three ... four ...

Hold the breath in your belly for another count of four. One ... two ... three ... four ...

Now slowly begin to let the breath out, either through your nose or mouth, whichever feels comfortable, to a count of four. One ... two ... three ... four ...

Now hold the breath out before you take another one. Hold it there for one ... two ... three ... four ...

Now breathe normally again, gently breathing in and out.

That completes your 16-second meditation. If that was your first ever meditation, congratulations! You are now officially a meditator. You are part of the cult! Send me your bank details immediately! And prepare yourself for the spaceship! Seriously, send me your bank details ...

It was pretty easy, wasn't it? Check back in with your body and mind. How do they feel compared to when we started a moment ago? What is your stress rating now? Any difference? Hopefully, you've slid down the scale a bit – if not to full Ryan Tubridy then maybe to Dáithí Ó Sé on his holidays in Kerry. Don't be disheartened if you don't feel any difference right away. This was your first attempt. Sometimes, if my mind is particularly busy, I'll run two, three or more 16-second meditations together. It just keeps the nice relaxed feeling coming and my mind in that present moment for longer. Remember, all we're trying to do is keep our minds in the 'now', guiding them away from worrisome or busy thoughts of things that might happen in the future and thoughts of the past that are potentially making us feel uncomfortable. When we find the centre, even for a few moments in a short meditation, we gift ourselves the potential for healing in our bodies and our minds.

One of the greatest things about the 16-second meditation is that it's also meditation 'to go'. You can bring it anywhere! You can use it in the queue for a chicken-fillet roll, while you're filling the petrol tank, on the train, in the car (keeping your eyes open, of course), in bed, on the golf course, even in the middle of a conversation. Have you ever sat chatting to someone who is pushing all your buttons and you feel like you may be on the verge of exploding? Simply breathe and count through the 16 seconds or belly breaths and the person you're talking to will never know what's happening. Remember, the technique powers down the amygdala, the part of your brain that wants to lash out, scream, run for the hills or bang the table. If you can have the presence of mind to do your 16-second meditation right in the heart of a difficult chat, you greatly lessen the chances of you flying off the handle.

Seriously, I do it all the time and nobody ever realises that I'm doing it. It just looks to the other person like I'm listening really intently. And not only am I meditating, but it also ensures that I keep my mouth shut for 16 seconds and do less damage. I've used it in arguments so I don't lose my cool unnecessarily. I've used it off-stage if I feel like nerves are getting the better of me. I've even used it in pay or contract negotiations to keep my head and speak my mind. If you have a speech or a presentation to make, a job interview, an important conversation with a loved one that you really want to go well, employing the 16-second technique before or during the event can stop your internal warning system from taking over the situation and leaving you wondering what happened when all the crazy monkeys in your head jumped out and wrecked the place.

We've all had that experience when we get carried away in a conversation, an encounter with a stranger or maybe in a work meeting where, afterwards, we're kicking ourselves that we didn't keep a cooler head. Or maybe it's hours after a confrontation and you're driving home or lying in bed thinking of all the really appropriate things you could or should have said. Meditation can give us that all-important distance from an experience, allowing us to think more clearly in an otherwise intense situation. It gives us the clarity of mind to react reflectively rather than reflexively and make better decisions in the moment. Whether we meditate in the actual moment or have created a practice that has prepared us for it in advance, we can bring our best, calmest selves to the experience. And we're far less likely to scream blue murder at our partner, cry at our desks or send our children to bed for playing with their peas at dinner.

Like the 16-second meditation, there are other forms of meditation that focus on counting the length of your breaths. By becoming aware of the lengths of our inhales and exhales, we enter a state of conscious breathing. This is where the breath is no longer just a passive activity that goes unnoticed. It becomes an anchor for our attention and helps to stop our mind flying all over the place like a rapidly deflating balloon. As the Zen Buddhist monk Thích Nhất Hạnh says, 'Breath is the bridge which connects life to consciousness, which unites your body to your thoughts. Whenever your mind becomes scattered, use your breath as the means to take hold of your mind again.'

There are quite a few techniques to choose from that can inspire conscious breathing. Remember that scene in *There's Something About Mary* where Ben Stiller's character, Ted, picks up the crazy hitchhiker? Played brilliantly by Harland

Williamson, the hitchhiker reveals a stunning business plan that he says is destined for success. Instead of the world-famous and hugely successful workout plan 8-Minute Abs, he has come up with the genius idea of going one better – 7-Minute Abs! And if you don't get the workout you need in seven minutes, he'll send you the extra minute – free! It's such a funny scene and it always makes me laugh. And that's how it seems sometimes when it comes to some meditations. There's the 4-5-6 Meditation, the 4-7-8 Meditation, the 7-11 Meditation , the 4-7-11 Meditation ... actually, maybe that's an aftershave. Anyway, there are many techniques where you use the breath and counting methods to relax your body and calm your mind. Despite the slight variations that our hitchhiker friend would be proud of, they all pretty much do the same thing. They stimulate the parasympathetic nervous system, as I mentioned. This is also known as the rest-and-digest state, which can be seen as the opposite of the fight-or-flight state we discussed. Our heart rate is low and steady, our blood pressure is no longer spiking and we feel nice and chilled out. I have a method I use, particularly if I'm struggling to get to sleep or get back to sleep after waking. I'm not even sure if it has a sexy name, so let's call it 4-to-10.

4-TO-10 MEDITATION

Start by getting nice and comfortable, either sitting or lying down.

Take a nice long, slow, deep breath in to your belly. Hold it in there for a moment. Then gently let it go, watching the breath as it leaves your body. As with all these techniques, we're breathing in through our nose and out through our mouth or nose, depending on what feels comfortable for you.

Let's do one more of those, shall we? A nice, long, slow, deep breath in. Feel your belly rise with the inhale. Hold it for a moment. Now let it go, watching the breath as it goes back out.

OK, now we're feeling nice and relaxed and we're ready to try 4-to-10.

When you're ready, breathe in to a count of four. Hold the breath for a moment. Now let the breath out to a count of five. When you get to five, pause for a few seconds before you take the next inhale.

Now breathe in for five. Hold for a moment or two. Now breathe out to a count of six. Pause again.

Breathe in for a count of six. Hold. Now breathe out for a count of seven. Pause again.

Breathe in for a count of seven. Hold for a moment. Breathe out gently to a count of eight. Pause again before inhaling.

Breathe in for a count of eight. Hold for a moment. Breathe out for a count of nine. Pause again.

Breathe in for a count of nine. Hold. Let the breath go for a count of ten. Pause.

Breathe in for a count of ten. Hold it here for the last time. Now let the breath out for a count of ten. Now breathe normally. Well done. Check in with yourself to see how you feel after that.

This may feel a bit clunky the first few times you do it. You may be straining towards the end as the count gets higher and the breaths get longer. But it will get easier, and pretty soon, you'll be challenging yourself on how slowly you can count to extend the breaths. Also, as I mentioned, your mind will always exercise its right to wander – it's what it does. You may find that when your brain is particularly busy, you get as far as six or seven in the meditation and suddenly you're thinking about a conversation at work or food you need to buy and you've totally lost your place in the breathing. When this happens to me, I go back to the start and begin again. This is not a form of punishment: it's a gentle form of practice.

Remember, we're training our brains to focus on the here and now, and each time our minds wander, it's an opportunity for more practice. It's kind of like mowing the lawn in our heads. We're trying to mow the grass in nice straight lines but every now and then, the lawnmower veers off course and disturbs the nice straight lines. So we go back to the start and begin mowing again. Don't beat yourself up if you lose your count in this breathing exercise – just see it as a game. You'll be surprised at how hard it is sometimes to keep your focus on the breaths and counting, but take comfort in the fact that everyone is the same and you're not doing it wrong. You've just been training your thoughts to jump all over the place for most of your life. Now it's time to get those playful puppies to 'sit'!

BODY/MIND MEDITATIONS

I use the following meditation any time I feel that stress has started to manifest in my body. Tension headaches, stiffness, mystery pains and general discomfort can be a sign that you need to help your body release some of the tension it's carrying around. We can go days on end without really connecting to our bodies in any meaningful way. They are amazing machines that patiently carry our consciousness around and allow us to do everything from skiing to sleeping. So often, though, we slip into a place where we seem separate from our bodies – until, that is, a problem arises somewhere in our physical being and suddenly our body is all we're thinking about. It's hugely beneficial to connect with our physical selves and a body scan is a wonderful way to do that. Many scientific studies show it can lower stress and anxiety and improve sleep.

Our bodies have a lot to tell us if we can make the time to listen. Often, a little ache or pain is a message from our body that something in our emotional or physical environment needs addressing. The simple act of breathing into our discomfort, wherever it manifests in the body, can be hugely effective in alleviating pain or stiffness caused as a result of unchecked tension or stress. In fact, mindfulness pioneer John Kabat-Zinn recommends the body-scan mindfulness technique as the most effective form of mindfulness meditation for pain conditions. So, whether you're experiencing a sore back or a weary mind, or you just want to fall asleep quicker, why not give this body-scan meditation a blast and see how it works for you. One of the great things about the body scan is that you can do it lying down. So get comfy!

THE BODY SCAN

Take a nice, long, slow, deep breath in through your nose. Hold it in your belly for a few moments and then gently let it go. Let's do another one of those. Another deep breath through your nose, into your belly, hold for a moment, now let it go.

Bring your attention to the top of your head. Imagine you're breathing into that space. Imagine your breath entering that place and, with each out breath, feel any stress or tension just drip away. Continue breathing in that way, letting your attention drift down to the sides of your head, your forehead, your cheeks, your jaw. With each breath in, you bring your attention to these places, and with each breath out, you feel the tension melt away.

Move your attention to your neck and shoulders. Spend a few breaths here, as we carry so much tension around in these areas, letting the stress melt away. Any time our mind wanders away from our scan, we gently bring it back to our body.

Continue scanning and breathing down the body. From the shoulders, move down the arms to the fingertips.

Breathe into the chest and back, down the torso and especially into the belly and lower back. With each breath, we release tension and stress, giving each part of our body the attention it deserves.

Breathing into the upper legs, the glutes, down to the knees, shins, ankles and feet. Breathing in, releasing with the out breath.

When we've reached the toes, do a final scan from bottom to top and top to bottom. See if you can find any place of discomfort or pain and breathe into it. Maybe it's not actual pain or stiffness, but a feeling or difficult emotion, possibly in your belly, chest or throat. Breathe into this space, feel the breath enter there and allow the feeling to release.

Take another couple of nice slow, long, deep breaths. When you're feeling ready, you can slowly open your eyes.

Even if you are feeling no real relief while doing this exercise, continue anyway. Its effectiveness does not depend on you feeling any tangible benefits in the moment. Simply do the meditation and try not to expect anything dramatic while you're doing it. It's an incredibly relaxing exercise and I hope you'll join me for my guided one when you feel the time is right.

In all these meditations so far, we have used the breath and counting the breath as our anchor to stop our thoughts flying off in different directions. For the next few, we're going to use something else to tether our thoughts – a mantra.

MANTRA MEDITATIONS

Up until now, we have looked at meditations where the focus of our attention is our breath. In some meditations, we can shift our focus from our breath to a mantra. A mantra is simply a word or a phrase that we repeat over and over again. Sometimes we say it out loud; sometimes we repeat it silently in our minds. It may seem new to you now but there's a good chance you've come across this kind of thing before. If you grew up Catholic, like me, you may remember Hail Marys being said in church. Growing up in Limerick in the 1980s, the Novena was a big deal.

This was a religious festival that took place every year and lasted for nine days during the summer. I remember cars driving around with luminous posters in their back windows advertising it, much like people do these days with stickers for their favourite radio stations. I remember as a child looking at the adverts dotted around the city that said 'Solemn Novena' and thinking, 'Why would anyone want to do something solemn?' It sounded like no craic at all. My parents were religious but not Novena-religious so I managed to avoid it for a while.

Around the age of 10, however, I was staying with a friend while my parents were away and Novenas were their thing. I was dragged along and it was a new experience. It was kind of like Mass, except for professionals. It was mostly old people who seemed lost in a dreamy mumbling session. There was call-and-answer-type arrangement where the priest would say half the Hail Mary and the congregation would fire back the rest, like some sort of religious tennis match. The rosary appeared to be a major part of it, and if you didn't have beads then you were clearly an amateur. I remember wondering how everybody seemed to know the words. There were extra prayers I'd never heard before and everyone seemed to have brought their praying A-game. No one was there for the doss. I had clearly been doing the Pass equivalent up until now – this was Honours Mass. I'm sure all those going got a lot out of it and felt they were getting one step closer to eternal peace, which made sense because, to me, it seemed to last an eternity. Finally, the mumbling stopped, we were set free and it was down to Sextons' shop for a packet of Fruit Gums and a copy of *Shoot!* magazine and all was right with the world.

Fast-forward 30 years and I'm sitting in a Buddhist retreat in that stronghold of hardcore Buddhist tradition – County

Cavan. I'm not particularly religious but I've always been curious about other traditions and expressions of spirituality. Maybe it's the altar boy in me, but I've always liked the rituals that go with these things, even in a regular Catholic church: the mysterious and overpowering smell of incense, the shiny chalices and ancient-looking golden ornaments and that wondrous ornate and secretive box that the priest opened with an oversized key – the tabernacle. I remember asking my mother at Mass what it was. She replied, 'That's where Jesus is kept,' meaning that's where they keep the communion host. I, however, pictured Jesus himself, lying down with his head towards the front like some sort of sliding morgue drawer you might see in an episode of *CSI: Miami*. I remember thinking he must be very bored just lying in there all day, waiting to be slid out for every Mass.

So I decided to give the Buddhist experience a go for the weekend, and it didn't disappoint in the ritual department. There was a feast of golden ornaments, incense, flowers, strange little stools, ornate pictures, cosy blankets and a monk in bright red and orange robes, all in a tumble-down old house in the back arse of Cyyyaaavaan.

At my first morning prayer session at 7 a.m., I found a meditation stool for myself and decided I would follow the lead of the regulars at the Jampa Ling retreat, who were very welcoming. Pretty soon the chanting started. I had the words in front of me but they were in ancient Sanskrit, so I didn't

really know what I was saying or how to pronounce anything properly – I channelled my inner mumbling Catholic
and that seemed to work. As we were chanting, being led by
the Tibetan monk in residence, I realised that, despite this
all being very strange and confusing, I had experienced this
kind of thing before. It was just like the Novena all those
years ago in Limerick. The monk said one thing, we replied
with another bit. Some people had beads, there was incense,
an altar, soft-glowing candles, a man in robes. It wasn't really
that different at all. And everyone seemed to be getting the
same thing out of it, with the same peaceful expressions
on their faces. There must be something else going on here
other than bead appreciation and incredible mood lighting.
And it turns out there was – breathing.

In 2001 a study took place in Pavia and Florence, Italy,
headed up by Dr Luciano Bernardi and his team of researchers.[13] The aim of the experiment was to examine the effects
on the body of engaging in rhythmic, repetitive prayer for-
mulas. Twenty-three participants were hooked up to monitors measuring the nervous system, blood flow, heart rate
and respiration. They were then made to recite a popular
Buddhist mantra, 'Om Mani Padme Hum', as well as the
original Latin version of the rosary, the Catholic prayer cycle
of the Ave Maria, in the same manner it is performed in
church. The scientists were surprised to find that recital of
both mantras created almost identical breathing patterns in

the participants of the study. Whether it was the Catholic rosary or the Buddhist prayer, each person's breathing slowed to six breaths per minute. Amazingly, this is also in line with Japanese, African, Native American and ancient Hindu prayer traditions. It seems that, consciously or unconsciously, every culture and tradition was creating the same patterns for prayer and breathing.

In his outstanding book *Breath*, tirelessly curious journalist James Nestor points out the truly wondrous effects this style of prayer-based mantra breathing had on the test subjects.[14] 'Whenever they followed this slow breathing pattern, blood flow to the brain increased and the systems in the body entered a state of coherence, when the functions of the heart, circulation and nervous system are coordinated to peak efficiency. The moment the subjects returned to spontaneous breathing and talking, their hearts would beat a little more erratically, and the integration of these systems would slowly fall apart. A few more slow and relaxed breaths, and it would return again.'

Simply put, the mumbling old people were on to something. They probably didn't know it in that Limerick church that day, but as they recited their prayers, answered the priest and fiddled with their rosary beads, their nervous systems, heartbeats and breathing patterns were all in glorious harmony and were creating the optimum environment for healing. Similarly, when I was out of my depth in the

Buddhist oasis in the heart of Cavan farmland, I was also creating harmony in my body and mind, even though I was repeating what seemed to me like gibberish. As the authors of the Italian study point out, 'the rosary might be viewed as a health practice as well as a religious practice', and the same can be said for any similar tradition that slows the breath to six breaths per minute.

They also suggest some other cultural explanations for similarities in the prayer practices of seemingly very different cultures and religions. 'Surprisingly, there is historical evidence for a link. The rosary was introduced to Europe by the crusaders, who took it from the Arabs, who in turn took it from Tibetan monks and the yoga masters of India. This supports the hypothesis that the similar characteristics and effects of these mantras and of the rosary may not be a simple coincidence.' Whatever the reason for the apparent crossover in spiritual traditions, the science shows it works to induce a calmer body and mind, something you're looking for or you wouldn't be reading this book ...

My favourite thing about this study is that it gives scientific credibility to one of the areas that can frighten people the most about all this meditation stuff – the 'woo woo' part. Most people are OK with the 16-second breathing and shrinking their amygdalas, but the minute there's the slightest sniff of chanting or strange prayers, they're out the door quicker than a hippie to a jar of hummus. It just conjures up too many images of baldy lads banging drums in the street, dreadlocked types trying to sell you lentil stew or possibly even that voodoo lad from that James Bond film with Roger Moore. From this study, however, and many subsequent ones involving the effectiveness of particular breathing patterns, we can see that there is more going on than a bunch of crusties filling time between dole collections. There are real, tangible changes to the body and brain taking place and, whether you're in your local church, in an ashram in India or sitting alone in your car repeating strange phrases to yourself, science tells us that this stuff works! You don't have to buy into the fashion, the rituals, the smelly candles or the food to reap the benefits of a mantra-based meditation practice. You just have to pick a mantra – a syllable, a word or a phrase that you're prepared to repeat, even if the meaning isn't clear to you – and take some time out for yourself to let it roam around your head for a while. If the ancient words and language are too 'out there' or if the religious aspects to the background of all this bring you out in a cold sweat, don't worry. I use English mantras all the time, with no religious connotations.

The same principles apply to a mantra meditation as they do to a breath-focused meditation. We bring our attention to the word or phrase we have in mind. When we realise that our mind has wandered, which it will, we gently guide it back to the mantra. So, let's try one.

The mantra used in this scientific experiment was 'Om Mani Padme Hum', pronounced om ma-nee pad-may hum. Seems like a good place to start. Translated to English, it roughly means 'praise to the jewel in the lotus'. This is a hugely simplified version, as we could probably spend the rest of this book debating all the possible roots and meanings of the phrase. The Dalai Lama has said its meanings are 'great and vast', as this one mantra is said to contain all the teachings of Buddhism. But there are many schools of thought that believe the literal meaning of a mantra is unimportant. They can be recited without ever focusing on the meaning, as it is the vibration of the words that contain the real benefit. If the word 'vibration' has you reaching for your bullshit bell, then simply remember the scientific study in Italy – it's the breathing pattern induced by this mantra that has such an amazing ability to calm the body and mind and bring all your systems into coherent alignment. If you're reading this book, you decided long ago to keep an open mind, so let's give it a go. If it's not for you, we'll move on to a simpler one and then to one in English that may be more your thing. There are many ways to recite this mantra but let's try this one.

OM MANI PADME HUM

Take a nice long, slow, deep breath in, through the nose, to your belly. Hold it for a moment; now let it go, slowly following the path of the breath back out.

Another nice long, slow, deep breath in through the nose. Hold it there, then slowly release it, following the path of the breath up and out of the body.

Now let's bring our attention to the mantra. Om Mani Padme Hum. Om Mani Padme Hum.

You can recite this out loud if you're comfortable to do so, you can whisper it to yourself or, if your partner is in the next room and you're concerned they will have you committed, repeat it silently in your mind.

Same rules apply – when your mind wanders, which it will, just notice that it has and gently guide it back to your mantra. Om Mani Padme Hum. Om Mani Padme Hum. Om Mani Padme Hum. Om Mani Padme Hum.

Just let the words come and go. As you repeat them, the words may become mixed up; they may get faster or slow down; you may forget what you're meant to be saying altogether. That's OK. Just guide your focus back to Om Mani Padme Hum each time you've wandered off.

Set a timer for five minutes and see how you go, just letting the phrase repeat over and over again. Om Mani Padme Hum.

Don't get hung up on doing it perfectly. Just give it a try. It's OK if you feel a bit foolish at first. Remember, I was so mortified when I began meditating, I couldn't even say it to my wife. Whatever happens, you will have taken time out for yourself and this is always healthy and helpful. They say the only bad meditation is the one you don't turn up for so give it a lash.

Om Mani Padme Hum.

'So Hum' is a powerful little meditation that uses the repetition of a mantra and all the beneficial effects of the breath to relax the body and calm the mind. 'So Hum' means 'I am' and I like this one as it reminds us that there's more going on inside ourselves than we show to the rest of the world. We all wear different hats each day: parent, partner, boss, employee, best friend, lover, sibling, carer. Some days we might play several different roles from moment to moment. These roles can be exhausting. It's easy to get caught up in them, and we can lose touch with that part of ourselves that's always underneath, that was there so naturally when we were kids. With so many of us working from home these days, the roles we play are becoming even more blurred. 'So Hum' allows us to focus on the deeper part of us that doesn't judge how we look, feel or behave. It just is.

As always with these mantras, you can ignore the meaning, if you like, and simply recite the words over and over again, using them as a simple anchor for your attention. If the 5,000-year-old language used in this mantras doesn't sit well with you, feel free to use the English translation, 'I am'. Lots of people find it easier to bring meaning and focus to the meditation if it's in English, so don't feel like you're doing the Pass version – it's just as effective! Find a comfortable spot once again and settle in. As my teacher always says, comfort is queen, so make sure you're comfy and warm and off we go.

SO HUM

Let's settle ourselves with a nice long, slow, deep breath in through the nose, right down into our bellies. Hold it for a moment, and then watch it go back out.

Another one of those, if you please, a nice long, slow, deep breath in. And gently let that go.

Allow your attention to drift to the mantra now, 'So Hum'/'I am'.

Take note of how you feel in your body and mind.

In this meditation, we're going to synchronise our breaths with the repetition of the mantra.

As you inhale, silently repeat the word 'So'.

As you gently exhale, silently say the word 'Hum'.

Keep doing this, one after the other, 'So' on the inbreath and 'Hum' on the exhale.

As always, your mind will be distracted by sounds inside and outside of the room. Your mind will be pulled away by physical sensations like gurgling tummies, crampy legs, itchy noses. When you've drifted from your mantra, don't beat yourself up – just guide your attention back to 'So Hum', allowing the breath to drift naturally and effortlessly in and out.

Set a timer for five minutes, or longer if you wish. When the time is up, gently release the mantra and sit for a minute or two, just following your breath in and out.

Well done. When you're feeling ready, give your fingers and toes a gentle wiggle and start to come back into the room. Check in with yourself once again and see how much more relaxed and calm you feel.

As I mentioned, if repeating the unfamiliar language has you arching your eyebrows into the middle of next week, worry not. An English mantra is just as effective. Remember, choosing a style of meditation is a personal thing and some things just won't sit right. When I was training as a teacher in California, we had very long and intense days of learning. We rose before the sun to meditate on the beach and worked well into the late evening. As the work was challenging and we were touching on some deeply personal things, my teacher had come up with a unique way of keeping everyone fired up when moods and energy began to wane.

One afternoon, he rose from his seat and uttered two words that would strike fear into the heart of any God-fearing Irishman – 'Dance break!' Now, I'm no shrinking violet. I will stand on any stage and act the eejit. Give me a microphone and I will bang out any U2 tune that comes to mind. But ask me to dance in front of strangers without a few drinks on board and I will curl into the foetal position and call for Mammy. And this was at lunchtime! Sober! In front of a gang of mostly women who seemed to be born without the kill-me-now gene. What made it worse was the dance breaks were being led by a twenty-something Hawaiian choreographer with hips that would make Shakira look like a newborn foal. She was snaking her perfectly tanned curves around the room like a sexy winding river to some kind of Latino hip-hop, whooping and clapping us all into action.

I did that awkward sway that men at weddings do for as long as they can muster before their wives eventually say, 'Oh, just go the bar, will ya?' I could feel my cheeks starting to redden and the sweat starting to come. What I didn't realise was that my teacher, the happy positive guy that he is, was filming all this for posterity and putting it directly on his Instagram Stories. Who sees the images straight away? Dave, my radio co-host back in Dublin. He couldn't be happier. When he eventually stops laughing, he reposts the hell out of it and tells everyone on the radio that I'm awkward day-dancing with a load of women in a sitting room in America.

My point is that there are parts of the meditation or 'spiritual' world that I'm not comfortable with at all. It makes me cringe and I want to laugh or run away. These things can tap into our inner cynic and the scoffing teenager inside us wants to point and say 'ha ha!' much like Nelson from the *Simpsons*. It was really interesting to me that, in spite of all the self-awareness, knowledge and confidence I had been gaining over the years through meditation, such a simple thing as dancing could flip a switch in me, trigger my fight-or-flight response and make me want to jump out the window.

There were many more dance breaks during my time there. One day, instead of my usual desire to internally freak out when the terrifying hip-hop started, I decided to actually try and feel my embarrassment. Like, really feel it, not push it away and escape as we all want to do when we're really uncomfortable. I swayed awkwardly and let the waves of 'get me out of here' just wash over me. I became aware of the sensations in my body: my rapid heartbeat, my sweaty palms, my churning stomach, my nervous laughter. I observed myself like a science experiment, and suddenly all the symptoms of 'dancebreakitis' started to ease off. I was overcome by a new wave of a different feeling. A feeling that was more 'ah, fuck it – who cares?' I began to embrace my awkwardness and my body loosened up and I started to move a bit more. I'm not ashamed to say I threw a few shapes. I 'shook a tackie', as they like to say in Limerick.

It might seem like a silly moment, really, but it reminded me of that day in school when I became the 'boy who turned purple'; that feeling I had where everyone's gaze felt like thousands of tiny pinpricks in my self-confidence. Sometimes those crazy, anxious, awkward, suffocating feelings and sensations we get when we're uncomfortable in a situation is just our sense of self looking to be heard. It's screaming, 'Some part of me feels threatened right now and I can't explain why but I'm going to do all these weird things in your body until you hear me! Hello? Hello, McFly!' Just allowing the signals of discomfort to come through is often enough to defuse them and send them on their way.

Often it may not be as dramatic as a big, sweaty, anxious moment. Maybe it's just an off feeling in your gut, a nagging restlessness or a heaviness in your heart. Ever seen a small child trying to get their mother's attention while she's chatting with a friend? They'll pull repeatedly on her trouser leg. 'Mammy. Mammy. Mammy.' It'll be quiet enough to begin with, but if Mammy isn't listening, it'll get louder and more intrusive. 'Mammy. Maaammmyyyy! MAAAMMMYYYY!' That's how the awkward, uncomfortable bits of ourselves get heard. If we don't listen in the beginning, they grow louder and more persistent. They'll talk to you through your body, through your mood, through your sleep. What was a sickly feeling in your tummy becomes a chronic condition. What were a few restless nights is now insomnia. What were a few pints is now falling down the stairs of a karaoke club …

Your 'I am' self will be heard, eventually. With meditation, we gradually learn the skill of listening to it sooner rather than later. We learn the skill of not trying to fix it immediately. That's not an easy thing to do. We have a such a trained need to fix anything that seems off. That's not always necessary. We can simply let it be noticed by finding some silence. However it manifests, hear it out. Don't rush to distract it away with telly or wine. Don't push back at it with anger or impatience. Try not to bury yourself in it with shame or guilt. Just let your body deliver the messages that are coming through. When we resist the urge to fix or repair and simply listen and be present with whatever is coming up for us, we create the space for real help to come in. Not only does meditation give us a chance to see what's really going on inside us, it also prepares us for the actions we must take as a result of those insights. From sitting in silence, we can gradually become aware that we need to make changes to our work, our relationships, our habits. Remember *Yogasthah kuru karmani*? By establishing ourselves in the present moment, we will then be in a calmer, more reflective, more stable state of mind to make whatever changes in our physical world are required.

What's your dance break? What's the situation or circumstance where your sense of self is calling for your attention? Once you've picked up on something that's bubbling up, take a few minutes to do this next meditation. I teach this to anyone who's struggling with their sense of self, anyone who's got something going on below the surface that won't leave them alone.

This is another mantra meditation. We repeat the phrase 'I trust' over and over again silently in our minds. Each time our mind wanders, we gently guide it back to our mantra: 'I trust'. This is an exercise to remind ourselves that we already have the resources we need inside us. We have an innate ability to deal with whatever is causing us discomfort. We've just forgotten about our inbuilt resilience because we have constantly been told that we are not enough, we don't have enough, we are not deserving enough. This mantra meditation does many things. It focuses your mind on your own ability to navigate challenges. We've got everything we need to deal with adversity but we sometimes forget to trust that part of ourselves that is beneath the surface, running the show, powering the ship.

'I TRUST' MEDITATION

Take a nice long, slow, deep breath in. Hold it in your belly for a moment. Gently let it go.

Let's go for another one of those. A nice long, slow, deep breath in through the nose, down into your belly. Hold it for a moment. Now, gently let it go, watching the breath travel up your body and out into the air.

Let's just watch our breath for a little while. Breathing in through the nose and down into the belly and then watching it go all the way back out. Feeling nice and relaxed now.

Let's silently repeat some phrases together to plant some seeds in that wonderful subconscious of yours.

'*I trust that I am stronger than I think.*'

'*I trust that I am stronger than I think.*'

'*I trust that I am stronger than I think.*'

'*I trust that I have everything I need to cope with whatever is troubling me right now.*'

'*I trust that I have everything I need to cope with whatever is troubling me right now.*'

'*I trust that I have everything I need to cope with whatever is troubling me right now.*'

'*I trust that the deeper part of me is wise and calm and knows what to do.*'

'*I trust that the deeper part of me is wise and calm and knows what to do.*'

'*I trust that the deeper part of me is wise and calm and knows what to do.*'

'*I trust that everything will work out for my greatest good.*'

'*I trust that everything will work out for my greatest good.*'

'*I trust that everything will work out for my greatest good.*'

Let's introduce our mantra. 'I trust'. Repeat it silently in your mind. 'I trust'. Let the words simply bubble up in your thinking. Some people like to see the letters of a mantra in their mind's eye. Others hear the sounds of the words. Whatever way the phrase comes in to your consciousness, go with that. As always, your mind will wander to sounds, physical sensations, things that have happened or might happen in the future. When you notice that your mind has

wandered, simply bring it back to the object of your attention
– your 'I trust' mantra.

Glance at your watch or set a timer on your phone for
five minutes. Gently repeat the phrase over and over again.
It may speed up in your mind; it may slow down. It may get
louder or quieter. Just stay with it and remember there is no
need to force it. Watch that furrowed brow. Meditation is not
straining: it's gently doing and allowing. Like a golf swing
or any other sporting skill, when we force it or tense up, it
doesn't come together so well. It's about finding a smooth flow
where it feels powerful but effortless. Anyone who plays golf
knows that this is easier said than done but give it a try!

'I trust ... I trust ... I trust ...' I'll check back in with you
in five minutes ...

Well done. Let's drop the mantra now and just breathe
normally. Check in with yourself to see how you're feeling.
Do you feel calmer? A little less anxious? Maybe you're feeling more relaxed and even a bit sleepy. The trusting space
can be a hard one to get into. When something is really
worrying us, it can feel like an impossible task to suddenly
switch off that part of our brain that desperately wants to
fixate on it. But I have found great relief from this simple
meditation.

On a comedy tour a few years back, I was feeling exhausted and quite overwhelmed by everything on my plate.
I was doing my radio show in the morning, then driving

across the country for live shows, then trying to arrive back home with the energy to be an attentive dad and husband. There seemed to be a level of performance I had to reach in everything and it was burning me out. Then I discovered 'I trust.' This simple little meditation was my lifeline and I looked forward to it every day. When I was in my hotel room before a live show, I lay on the bed and did this meditation. If I didn't feel any better, I would lean in to it a bit more and do another ten minutes, and another and another, until I felt my nervous system starting to relax. It was a great reminder that I had the strength to do all the things that I had planned.

I trusted in the excitement that led me to embark on a comedy tour in the first place. I trusted in my ability to entertain all the people who had bought tickets to see me perform. And I trusted that if I had bitten off more than I could chew and was taking on too much work, then I would know how to make adjustments and plan better in the future. Just knowing that I had all the tools I needed already, right there within me, was a great relief, and it's something we often forget. 'I trust' shines a spotlight on those parts of us that are ready and waiting to climb aboard and lend a hand when we're under pressure, feeling anxious or doubting our ability to navigate the challenges we have coming our way. It gives us a quiet place in which to find strength and comfort, and, best of all, it only takes a few minutes.

I realise reading the meditations on the page could be a bit distracting but I just want to introduce you to some different techniques so that when you listen to the guided meditations included with this book they will seem a bit familiar to you. In the meantime, let's look at another style that brings your imagination out to play – visualisation.

VISUALISATION MEDITATION

Visualisation meditation has been used by our favourite sports stars for decades. Golfing greats Tiger Woods and Jack Nicklaus both extolled the virtues of visualisation for helping to reach the dizzying heights of sporting success that they have both enjoyed. According to Nicklaus, he 'never hit a shot, not even in practice, without having a very sharp in-focus picture of it in my head'.[15] Tiger used to say he could still see the target even when he was looking at the ball and often imagined the ball going through invisible windows in the air.[16] Legendary boxer Muhammad Ali's secret weapon was his 'future history'. This was his particular style of visualisation where he would imagine himself standing in the ring after a bout, hand raised in the air by the referee, enjoying all the minute details of the moment in his mind. He would see the camera flashes, feel the sweat on his brow, immerse himself in the feelings of victory and enjoy the smiles of his supporters and loved ones.

The mind is such a powerful tool when we use it to mentally rehearse outcomes or situations where we wish to bring our best selves to the table. There are parts of our brain that cannot tell the difference between real or imagined events, and when we can tap into this grey area in our minds and witness our full potential before it actually happens in the physical world, the chances of us performing like absolute ledgebags vastly increases.

Oprah Winfrey credits the landing of her role in the famous film *The Colour Purple* with months of visualising herself as the successful actress she wanted to be. After reading the book, she became obsessed with being in the film if it was ever made. So she set about visualising herself in the role that would eventually lead to her Oscar nomination for Best Supporting Actress.

She recounts the inspiring tale of when she finally got to audition for the part of Sofia and found herself reading opposite her on-screen husband, Harpo. Harpo is Oprah backwards. She knew something was working in her favour and took it as a sign from a higher power that she was on the right path. Her production company is also called Harpo Productions. Whether you believe all that to be a divine sign or pure coincidence is up to you. And, if your name happens to be Tom Red (Dermot backwards) then you're probably freaked out by now. My point is, visualisation is a proven tool of many outstanding people who have done things that seem impossible to a lot of us.

But it's not just celebrities who have benefited from these techniques. A study from Loyola Marymount University in California showed dancers could increase their jumping heights by visualising their body as a spring.[17] One of the most mind-boggling bits of research, however, is a 2004 study from the Cleveland Clinic in Ohio.[18] It took a group of healthy young adults and divided them into three smaller groups. Over a period of twelve weeks, they engaged in a visualisation technique for fifteen minutes a day, five days a week. Group one imagined that they were working out their little finger. That's my kind of workout! Group two imagined they were working their bicep muscle. The third group actually trained in the gym. Groups one and two were told to merely imagine moving their muscles but without touching or moving them. The researchers measured their strength before, during and after the visualisation exercises.

After the twelve weeks were up, they received the data. Group one, who had mentally trained their little fingers, had increased their strength in those muscles by 35 per cent! The second group, who had imagined working their biceps, increased their strength in those larger muscles by 13.5 per cent, while the actual training group's finger strength rose by 53 per cent. This showed that ordinary gym-goers could increase their strength by a considerable amount simply by imagining the workout. Why do they never tell us this when we're signing up to a gym? Brain activity measurements in the study showed that the participants vastly improved the communication between the brain and the muscles involved, just by repeatedly visualising the physical movements. Even better news is that it's not an age-dependent phenomenon. The research also proved effective with elderly participants.

This all points to something very important – intention. It's so common for us to drift through each day, never really imagining or deciding how we want to feel or what we would like to see unfold. We move around like those automated vacuum cleaners that bounce from one obstacle to another, never planning how we would actually like to navigate our experience. Actually, my know-it-all teenage son has just explained to me that these little vacuum cleaners are called Roombas and actually do plot out their journeys in advance, using artificial intelligence to map out the landscape of your entire house. So, let's go with a pinball analogy for now and he can consider himself grounded.

We've all seen a pinball machine where the balls bounce randomly off things, flying around in every direction. It looks chaotic and unpredictable and sometimes, more balls appear from nowhere and join the madness. In order to keep things in motion, we hammer the flippers to keep as many balls in the game as possible before they inevitably disappear down the chute. So many of our days are spent like this, flapping around, trying to keep things in some kind of coherent motion. It can be exhausting at the best of times and leaves us feeling helpless and very far away from a personal high score. Visualisation, though, allows us to lessen the chances of being mindlessly buffeted from one experience to another as we go through our day. The positive benefits of visualisation are said to be plentiful, including increased focus and performance, lower levels of stress and anxiety, better sleep, more confidence and alleviation of pain.

When we use visualisation in our meditations, instead of keeping our attention on our breath or a mantra, we use mental images as our anchor to focus our mind. Depending on what we are hoping to achieve, any number of scenarios can be played out in the stillness of our meditation. If we are hoping to heal our bodies, we may focus on images of the body attacking disease or being healed by light. If we are looking to reach goals in our work or sport, we could bring to mind images of what success might look like in that scenario. If we are hoping to relax and find more calm, then we could use the image of a peaceful garden or other location as the focus of our attention. How you imagine your goal is really up to you. One person's mental oasis could be another's bad dream so settle on imagery that works for you. Feel free to tweak it so it fits in with your ideal mental landscape.

The most important part of a visualisation meditation is, I believe, feeling. Not only are we trying to teach our subconscious what we want to see and witness in the hours or days ahead, we are also showing it how we want to feel. It's the difference between seeing a two-dimensional drawing on a piece of paper and getting the full three-dimensional experience. The more components we can add to the desired experience, the more strands our subconscious has to grab onto. The more real we can make the experience in our minds and bodies during a meditation, the more familiar it becomes, and reaching that state beyond the meditation becomes more likely. As well as seeing the adoring crowd applauding him in his visualisations, Muhammad Ali was feeling the elation of victory, the confidence and strength in his body, the joy of sharing the experience with loved ones. As his famous quote goes, 'If I can conceive it, and my heart can believe it, then I can achieve it.'[19] When we visualise, we bring in every component of the experience so that the whole thing can be fully witnessed, fully expressed and fully enjoyed. Then our subconscious mind has everything it needs to recreate the experience in our physical world.

A fascinating study carried out by Australian psychologist Alan Richardson nicely demonstrates the importance of using as many senses as possible in a visualisation meditation.[20] Richardson took a group of basketball players and divided them into three groups to test their ability to make free throws – shooting a hoop from the free-throw line without anyone interfering with them. The first group practised free throws every day for a period of twenty days.

The second practised free throws on just the first and twentieth days. The third group also practised free throws on the first and last days of the study but spent an additional 20 minutes every day *visualising* making free throws. The results of the study were pretty astounding. Those who only practised twice over the twenty days, unsurprisingly, showed no improvement. The group that practised every day improved by 24 per cent. The players, however, who only physically practised two days but also visualised free throws every day improved by 23 per cent – almost as much as those who really practised! Richardson added one other important thing, though, in his paper published in *Research Quarterly*. The most effective visualisation occurred when the players did more than just 'see' the ball going into the hoop. Their results improved when they also 'felt' the ball in their hands and 'heard' the ball bouncing on the ground. The more elements they added, the better the outcome. So adding in all our senses can dramatically affect the power of a visualisation. Let's try one so you get an idea of what's involved.

SACRED SPACE VISUALISATION

Get nice and comfy. Turn off your devices or put them on Do Not Disturb. Take a long, slow, deep breath in through the nose. Hold it for a moment, then gently let it back out.

Take another long, slow, deep breath in. Hold it in your

belly. Then gently let that go. Really good.

Let's just watch our breath for a minute or so as our body finds a restful state and the outside world gets quieter.

When you're ready, we're going to create a safe, sacred space for ourselves. I'd like you to pick a place in your mind that represents security and peace. It could be a cosy cottage in the trees, a house by the sea, a castle at the top of a mountain or lying out underneath the stars. Maybe it's a peaceful and beautiful garden filled with flowers of all colours. Perhaps it's the simplest of rooms with a crackling fire. This is a space just for you. It's your private place to come and go as you please, where no one can interrupt or bother you. All the swirling busyness of the world can't reach you here, and it's yours to enjoy as long as you like. If you have any difficulty imagining such a place, choose a place from your childhood or your recent past that represents feeling happy and content. I tend to imagine the fourth tee box in Lahinch Golf Club, so it really can be anywhere! When you have created the image in your mind, imagine you are there and begin to witness your surroundings.

Let's begin with what you can see. What do you see around you? Are there decorations or pictures of loved ones? If you are out in nature, what plants, trees or animals do you see? Is it night time or day time? Can you see stars in the sky or the dance of firelight on the wall?

Try to take in as much detail as possible. If you find it

difficult to pick out particular details and it's more just a sense of being somewhere, don't worry, just go with what your imagination is showing you.

Next let's bring our attention to the sounds in our safe environment. Can you hear the wind outside? Are there birds singing or animals making noises? Can you hear the crackle of a fire or the crashing of waves? Try to focus your mind on what sounds you can hear right now in this visualisation. Any time some real-world sounds distract you, just bring your attention back to the world of your sacred space. Perhaps your ideal spot is totally silent, far away from the noises of everyday hustle and bustle. Maybe you can only hear the sound of your own peaceful breathing. Sit with those sounds for a few more moments.

Now let's interact with the environment a bit more. Let's see what we can touch and feel around us. Can you pick up and examine anything? Are there ornaments or keepsakes from happy times? Can you feel the bark of a tree or soft grass or sand under your feet? Can you take a cool paddle in crystal-clear water? Is there something to eat or drink that feels tasty and satisfying? Focus on the sensations that your surroundings can offer for a little longer.

Now let's bring our attention to the smells around us. Maybe the air smells fresh and salty. Perhaps the lush smells of a forest or garden surround you, or maybe you can smell baking or food being prepared. Allow the smells to form in your imagination. If you're struggling with this part, just stay focused on the peace and calm in this special place.

Now we bring our attention to how we really feel. This is your special, sacred place that you have created for yourself. Try to zone in on the nice feelings you have here and really feel them in your body. If you feel rested and calm, then breathe deep into your belly, feeling that peace and calm enter your body. Are you feeling happy or confident? Do you feel strong and healthy? Whatever comes to mind, really immerse yourself in that emotion, breathing it in deep each time and basking in how it feels in your mind and body. If it helps, place your hand wherever you feel the centre of that emotion, like on your heart, solar plexus or belly. Feel the breath supercharging that feeling and planting it wherever you feel it's directing you.

Now just enjoy all the sensations and emotions of the special, personal space you have created. Spend a few more minutes here, experiencing all there is to discover in this wonderful place. Wander around, sit in silence, have a sleep, say a prayer, whatever comes to mind – it's entirely up to you. And, as always, whenever you become distracted by physical sensations or thoughts in your actual environment, just guide your attention back to the safe place in your meditation. You may also want to introduce a mantra such as 'I am safe,' 'I am blessed,' 'I am happy' or 'I am healthy' – whatever feeling you'd like more of in your life, feel free to say it quietly in the safety of your personal meditation space.

When you feel you've spent enough time there, you can

begin to let it go. Have one last look around, offer up some gratitude for the creation of the space and then see yourself leaving calmly and quietly. You are bringing all the positive emotions you fostered here with you and you know you can return here anytime you wish.

Let's finish the journey, still keeping our eyes closed and taking a nice long, slow, deep breath in. Hold it in for a moment and gently let the breath go.

Let's do one more of those. A nice long, slow, deep breath in, hold it in your belly and gently let that go.

Give your fingers and toes a wiggle and feel yourself coming back into the room where you are. And when you're totally ready you can gently open your eyes.

Well done! Now let's do a visualisation meditation for some particular goal in your life. No matter what you're trying to achieve, we use the same technique. We zone in on the imagery but, more importantly, we focus on the feelings and sensations that reaching our goal will achieve. This could be a meditation to deal with nerves around public speaking. Maybe you want to play the game of your life in a particular sport. Perhaps you're hoping to meet the right person or get the right job. Anything that you're trying to achieve can be the focus of your attention in this meditation. Remember, this isn't magic – it still requires you to take steps towards your goals in real life. It does, however, focus your attention on what you want so that you can move towards that destination without getting pushed and pulled in every direction like the pinball we spoke about earlier. And science proves that effort plus visualisation creates better performance and higher achievement. So what have you got to lose?

GOAL VISUALISATION

Take a nice long, slow, deep breath in through the nose. Hold it there for a moment. Now gently let that breath go.

And another nice long, slow, deep breath in. Hold it in your belly for a moment. Now gently let that go. You're feeling nice and relaxed now. You've nowhere else to be and nothing else to do for these few minutes that you have made time for in your day.

Let's deepen our thinking now before we slide into our visualisation. Let's silently ask the question 'Who am I?' Repeat that silently in your mind. 'Who am I?' We're moving beyond the surface opinions we may have about ourselves or that we think other people have about us. By asking 'Who am I?' we remind ourselves that there is much more to us than the masks we wear each day or the image we portray to those around us all the time. We will be using that deeper part of ourselves to fuel the power of our visualisation right now. Let's spend one more minute asking 'Who am I?'

OK, now bring your attention back to your breathing, watching your breath coming in and going back out. Really good.

Now we're going to focus on the thing that you want to achieve or go well. Let an image of how you would like it to unfold come to your mind. See yourself standing where you want to be. Who is around you? What kind of place is it? Look around – what can you see? If details are sketchy or you don't know exactly what outcome you would like, then focus instead on how you want to feel. See yourself in the flow, with everything happening effortlessly. Feel the joy in your body; breathe it into your chest and your belly. Imagine you have just completed the task and feel uplifted and proud of yourself. See yourself looking at yourself in the mirror – the look on your face is one of total pride and joy. You are smiling and laughing at how easily you achieved your goal. See people congratulating you. How do their hugs and handshakes feel? If you are visualising meeting the right person, how does it feel to be with them? Don't be concerned if you don't have details of their face – just go with the feeling of being with them.

Let's spend a few minutes really letting these positive emotions sink in and nestle into our very core. We are planting subconscious seeds, and the emotions we feel are the water that will help them to grow. Let yourself bask in these feelings and images like you are seeing yourself as the star of your own movie.

When you are ready, you can release those images and feelings. Let's lock in those positive and fulfilling experiences with a nice long, deep breath into our bellies once again. Hold it in for a moment or two and gently watch the breath go back out.

One more of those. A nice long, slow, deep breath in, holding for a moment, then letting the breath go back out.

Now we offer just a little bit of gratitude for the imagined experience we had, taking one more long breath in and letting it go.

You can start to move your fingers and toes as we come back into the room and, only when you're feeling ready, we slowly open our eyes.

Well done. That is a very powerful exercise which, when done regularly, is scientifically proven to enhance your chances of success.

MEDITATIONS FOR OTHERS

Sometimes meditation seems a bit 'me, me, me!' We're all sitting there, trying to calm our nervous systems, improve our sleep, visualise our goals and make ourselves into the greatest, most balanced versions of ourselves possible. Doesn't that all appear a bit ... well, selfish?

It could seem that way until you think about something I touched on earlier – the ripple effect. The idea is that every aspect of our behaviour has an effect on the people and situations around us. If we are bringing a version of ourselves that is angry, anxious, impatient or mean-spirited, this will ripple out into all our interactions and experiences. If you've ever worked with an 'office grump', you'll know what I'm talking about. Everyone feels the effect of someone in the group who is bringing negativity to the table every day. Obviously, we will all have bad days, days where our ripple is lacking positivity, but I'm talking about the ripple effect of people whose individual perspective on life has a real impact on the feelings and moods of people around them. Maybe there's someone in your home whose ripple you're struggling with. Maybe you feel that *your* ripple is causing stress or discomfort to those around you. When we take time to do a bit of emotional balancing for ourselves, we affect our ripple.

If we are practising meditation or breathing techniques, like the 16-second meditation above, and are finding we manifest a calmer, kinder, more empathetic version of ourselves, then that will have a direct effect on the people we spend the most time with, and most probably a more positive one. One of the main reasons, therefore, that we meditate is to improve the quality of our ripple into the lives of the people we care about the most. Just as you drop a stone into water and the waves radiate outwards, we can send out helpful, positive energy or destructive, unhelpful and hurtful stuff. So the work we do on ourselves through meditation is anything but selfish. It's the opposite. By merely allowing our best, most natural selves to emerge, we automatically improve the well-being of others around us. So be selfish and meditate for your own good – it's the most thoughtful thing you can do for others!

Sometimes, we may just feel like we would like to send positivity towards someone we know. Maybe a friend is going through a health challenge or a child is struggling at school. Perhaps someone you know is hurting from a relationship or someone you love is far away and you wish them well. Maybe you'd like to show your support to a cause you feel is worthwhile by meditating on their behalf. Whatever the reason, it can be a very positive and often reassuring thing to offer a meditation for someone other than ourselves: in steps the loving-kindness meditation. If the 'loving-kindness' title has you reaching for the sick bag, hold that pukey thought. This little meditation comes laden down with scientific credentials. Studies over the last 15 years have shown regular use of loving-kindness meditations have the following benefits:[21]

- increases positive emotions like joy, pride, hope, contentment, happiness and love
- improves life satisfaction
- decreases depressive symptoms
- improves social connection
- lowers chronic pain
- decreases PTSD symptoms
- raises empathy and compassion

- decreases migraines and helps with migraine pain
- curbs self-criticism
- makes you kinder to yourself and others

Research also shows that this meditation can even help slow biological ageing. A 2013 study looked at the telomeres of participants who regularly practised loving-kindness meditations.[22] Telomeres are part of your genetic material, or chromosomes, that act as markers for biological ageing: the longer your telomeres, the younger your body. Stress is known to reduce the length of telomeres and cause us to age quicker. Researchers found that women with experience of loving-kindness meditation had longer telomeres than a control group and showed less signs of ageing. Loving-kindness, as airy-fairy as it sounds, was actually making them younger. Why don't they ever tell us this in those adverts for face creams? Instead of some model slathering her airbrushed skin with ridiculously expensive serum, they should show her sitting down with her eyes closed taking a deep breath. Why? Because she's worth it ... And it's waaay cheaper. So let's see what's involved.

This meditation comes from the Buddhist practice of 'metta bhavana', which is from the ancient Indian language of Pali. *Metta* means 'loving-kindness' and *bhavana* means development or cultivation. So the practice encourages a sense of love (the non-romantic kind), friendliness and kind-ness. We start by focusing on ourselves and then we move outwards towards other people in our lives. This version has elements of the Buddhist tradition, of my teacher, Davidji, and of my own. It's what I like to do and I hope you like it too. It's especially helpful if you are feeling any kind of anger, frustration or grievance towards somebody. So tell the kids to go play in the traffic for a few moments and let's give it a go.

METTA BHAVANA

Get comfy wherever you are. Take a nice long, slow, deep breath in through the nose. Hold that in your belly for a moment and then let it gently go.

Let's try another one of those. A nice long, slow, deep breath in. Hold. And gently follow the breath back out. Really good. You're getting relaxed already, feeling the tension start to drip away from your body.

First, we're going to breathe in some of that metta, that nice loving-kindness. Breathe deep into your heart and, with each breath, I'd like you to imagine feelings of peace, calm and tranquillity. With each breath in we're breathing in calm and letting that settle in our chest. With each breath out, we let go of any stress or tension that we're hanging onto in our bodies. We're letting in those positive emotions now and beginning to feel joy, confidence and strength. With each breath the positive feelings grow and we let go of any stress with each breath out. If it helps, you can imagine a golden light entering your body and bringing with it a great feeling of warmth and comfort.

Next, let's begin repeating the phrase 'may I be well and happy'. Let the phrase settle in your mind and begin to feel a feeling of love and warmth grow in your chest. Let that phrase and feeling build for a little while longer. Well done. Now we're ready to begin sending that metta or loving-kindness back out.

Picture your loved ones, either alive or who have passed. It may be family, a special teacher or guide, a relative, someone from your past or present. Take a long, slow, deep breath and, as you breathe out, imagine you are sending back out all that warmth and kindness that you have been building in yourself. You can imagine a light coming from you and showering them. Offer the phrase 'may you be well and happy'. Repeat this several times while picturing them in your mind.

Next think of your friends. Take a long, slow, deep breath in and, as you breathe out, send your friends all those positive, powerful feelings. Do this several times and repeat the same phrase on their behalf: 'May you be well and happy.'

Now, think of someone you know who is suffering. Maybe they're under pressure financially, maybe they're stressed about work. Perhaps they are struggling with a health challenge. Wish them well and send them love, radiating from you to them.

Next, think of someone you have no particularly strong feelings about, someone neutral. This could be a neighbour you don't know very well, someone you see on the train every day, maybe someone at work who you don't talk to very often. Take a deep breath and imagine you are sending them loving-kindness. 'May you be well and happy.'

Then, take another nice deep breath, fill your chest with loving-kindness and this time send some of that metta to someone with whom you have a grievance. This can be a challenging one. You don't have to forgive them, just send them light and love.

Continue widening the circle and picture the whole earth as a globe in front of you. Imagine all the people on the earth and, with a long, slow, deep breath in, breathe in all the loving-kindness you can muster, and then, as you breathe out, imagine all your light and love spreading across the globe, touching the hearts of everyone on it.

Finally, imagine you are sending loving-kindness out beyond the earth. Picture the vast array of galaxies and send your metta there, right to the far corners of the universe.

Now just bask in the sea of loving-kindness that you have created. Feel it as waves radiating outward from you and returning from everywhere you sent it. Sit with this feeling for a few more minutes. When you feel ready, allow the meditation to come to an end and slowly open your eyes.

Well done.

* * *

Now you have experienced a good selection of types of

meditation. Many of my guided meditations contain elements of all of the above. If your head is spinning a bit at present, don't worry. You've just seen the whole menu and there's no pressure to eat everything. As you try the guided meditations, it will become second nature to you and you'll find your sweet spot. As I said previously, meditation is like listening to music. You try out different styles until you find one that resonates with you. Personally, I like using a mantra when I meditate. It seems easier for me to latch onto for some reason. My wife prefers a guided meditation with a voice that doesn't wreck her head. Try them all out, mooch around, dig into the apps, discover different teachers, try the free ones with this book and beyond. We are all different, coming from different places and paces, and need to hear different things from different people at different times. So don't worry if it feels a bit clumsy or clunky at first: you will find your groove and that healing peace and silence will come out to meet you.

CHAPTER 10

HOW TO MAKE SURE YOU DON'T BECOME CRAP AND FORGET TO DO IT

have a beautiful Fender Telecaster electric guitar. It's a lovely off-white colour. It's the kind of off-white colour that would make the lads who make up names for house paint very excited. If they were trying to come up with a name for the colour of my guitar, they'd probably choose titles like 'Calm Cottage', 'Satin Slipper' or 'Creamy Delight'. Actually, the last one sounds a bit gross. But I love this guitar. I love how it looks, how it sounds, how the smooth neck feels in my hand. And I never play it. Like, never. It sits in my mancave like an expectant child waiting for me to pick it up and play with it, but I never do. Sometimes, I look at it and feel guilty. I think of how I dragged Dave to several guitar shops to find just the right one. I was so full of intention and hope. 'I'm really going to apply myself this time.' 'I'm going to get lessons and finally be able to pick up a guitar and play something other than "Wonderwall".' Oh, and my particular favourite: 'By this time next year, I'm going to have finished my own album!'

I got lessons for a while. My boys and I began learning at the same time from the same teacher. This was a terrible idea. Any time I tried to give out to them for not practising, they would just say, 'But, Dad, you haven't practised either!' A quick 'Go to your room' would generally end that debate quite efficiently. Like any self-respecting man, I bought all the expensive attachments: cables, amps, loop pedals, mics, effects units. I had a dream that I would make an album that channelled all of my early nineties shoe-gazing and grunge sensibilities into one epic masterpiece. I had day-dreams about the reviews:

'This album has blindsided the music industry. It's raw, powerful and brings together all the strands of rock that have been forgotten in a sea of factory-produced pop. And what's more, this guy is in his forties!' *NME*

'Who is this Dermot Whelan? We don't know but we want more!' *Hot Press*

'Even though he only seems to know four chords, he makes them work!' *The Irish Farmers Journal*

But the album never materialised. My eagerness gave way to long bouts of 'meh' and the guitar's shade became less 'Satin Slipper' and more 'Forgotten Old Boot'. The reason my chances of appearing on Jools Holland had dwindled so rapidly was simple – I never turned up to do the work. I dabbled in it, I tuned it a lot, I arranged it so it looked just right in the room and I talked about it quite a bit. But that's as far as it went. Meditation works the same way. So many of us want so dearly to have a meditation practice that we can rely on, that makes us happier, that keeps us calm, that lightens our load. But, like anything else, good intentions only get you so far and, like that difficult first album, they only materialise into something worthwhile if we put the work in. It's very hard to dabble your way into a habit. It takes time, commitment and, the most important element of all, turning up.

My local gym has inspirational phrases written on the wall. I never paid much attention to them when I was in there but one always stood out: 'The only bad session is the one you didn't turn up for.' I always thought, pedantically, it should have said, 'The only bad session is the one for which you didn't turn up,' but I can see why it mightn't have had the same impact … There is, however, truth to this bit of clichéd gym graffiti, and it applies just as effectively to meditation. All the science we chatted about earlier points to one thing – regular use of meditation. Only when we apply ourselves to doing it daily do we start to see those scientifically proven benefits.

I realise this might sound like a bit of a buzz-killing teacher's approach, but I want to save your meditation practice from becoming my poor guitar. Meditating every day, no matter how clumsy, uncomfortable, unsuccessful or useless you feel at it, is the only thing that will make it work for you. Sure, there are breathing tips and tricks that we have learned that will help you in moments of stress or challenge, but to start to feel the deeper, tangible, life-changing benefits that come with finding stillness and silence in your day, you have to turn up for your daily session. Even if that session is just 16 seconds long, doing it daily gets results. I know this because I've been there. As I said earlier, I ended up sobbing in a GP's office because, despite all the wonderful tools and stress-busting information available to me, I was just talking about meditation and not actually doing it.

You know those guys in the gym who spend their whole time talking and drinking protein shakes but never actually doing any training? I was the meditation equivalent of that. And it meant I wasn't switching off my stress response. I wasn't stopping the barking guard dog or the ringing alarm inside me. So the stress tide never went out and I got burnt out. Many of us get this concept when we think of physical fitness. No one expects to go to the gym twice or three times a month and get ripped. It's just not going to happen. So if we want to train those parts of our brain that keep us calm, clear-headed, present and making better decisions, then we have to do the reps and keep turning up. And the good news is, there are things we can do to help make this process as effortless as possible.

CREATE A ROUTINE

When I give a talk, I always ask, 'Who here has tried meditation before?' Most of the hands go up. 'Who here has tried meditation and has managed to keep the practice going?' Most of the hands go back down again. This is part of being human. We have busy lives full of things to do, places to be and people to care about. Our days already feel jam-packed so to try and fit in something else can feel like a challenge. We are, however, creatures of habit, and when we can build something into our daily routine, it no longer seems like a chore or an added extra and we are far more likely to do it the next day, and the next and the next.

My teacher, Davidji, gave me three letters that were pivotal in managing to keep my meditation going – RPM. These stand for Rise, Pee, Meditate! This process simplified everything for me. The idea behind RPM is that you get up, do what you gotta do in the bathroom and then sit down to meditate before you take a look at your phone or do anything else. The temptation to look at emails, news websites, WhatsApp and everything else is so strong when we wake up, and this process ensures we don't allow those things to influence our state of mind before we set ourselves up for the day.

A University of Sussex study, published in 2011, has shown that exposure to negative news can have a direct impact on our mood, increasing feelings of sadness and anxiety.[23] The research also showed that watching negative news can even make us feel worse about our own worries and concerns, which are totally unrelated to the content we watch! So we want to make sure that we don't let outside influences affect our stress levels before we get a chance to establish some balance first thing in the morning.

By meditating before we immerse ourselves in all the clutter of the day, there will also be fewer distractions during meditation itself. Fewer emails mean fewer wandering thoughts about them; fewer bad news stories mean fewer fearful or anxious thoughts pulling you away from your breath or your mantra. That first half hour after waking is so precious and gives us the opportunity to 'set the table' for the day ahead. And what we do with that half hour can have a real impact on how we feel our day goes.

A 2015 Harvard study carried out in conjunction with author and entrepreneur Ariana Huffington, showed that watching just three minutes of negative news in the morning made viewers 27 per cent more likely to report having a bad day six to eight hours later.[24] In other words, at the end of their day, those who had been exposed to the equivalent of a short negative news video first thing in the morning were far more likely to report their day not going well than those who had not watched the same news. It is important to point out, however, that not all news is bad news. The same study found that those who watched transformative, solution-focused news had a completely different response. They were shown stories of resilience, of overcoming the odds, such as inner-city kids studying hard to succeed in a school competition or a 70-year-old man finally passing an exam after years of trying. Those who watched these kinds of news stories first thing in the morning reported having a good day 88 per cent of the time. It's clear, therefore, that, just like what we eat affects how our bodies respond, whatever we put into our minds first thing in the morning has a real impact on our moods and the perception of our day. Practising the RPM method, even if it means setting the alarm clock for 10 or 15 minutes earlier, can transform how we feel our days are going. And how we feel our days are going is, over time, how we feel our life is going.

I'm often asked what is the right amount of time to meditate for when practising in the morning. The answer is what you can manage and what you can keep doing every day. Often, beginners will set out with the best intentions of doing half an hour every morning. Soon, though, this is too much to maintain, so the time gets shorter and shorter until it disappears altogether and the busyness of the morning swamps everything once again. If 16 seconds is all you can manage at first but it allows you to keep coming back to it each day, then start there. Then try a minute, five minutes; just keep turning up. If a ten-minute guided meditation is what works for you then do that. Just like any fitness regime, the most successful one is the one that you can maintain, and it's the same for your meditation practice.

Us humans love a routine, particularly in the morning. We get up at the same time and we tend to do everything in the same order: have a shower, get dressed, make our coffee, drive the same way to work. When we can drop a self-care practice like meditation into that morning routine, before we ever leave the house, it becomes second nature and we don't really have to think about it. What a lovely feeling it is to pull the front door behind you in the morning, step into your home office or wave the kids off to school knowing that, despite the earliness of the day, you have already banked something really positive for yourself that you know is scientifically proven to make you feel happier and more fulfilled. Rise, Pee, Meditate!

The sequel to RPM is RAW. They're a bit like the movies *Home Alone* and *Home Alone 2: Lost in New York*. Both are very respectable by themselves but they're so much better together! (We never speak of *Home Alone 3, 4* and *5*. Never.) RAW stands for Right After Work. The idea is that we're giving ourselves a kind of emotional shower, rinsing away all the stress and clutter we may have picked up across the day. By the time five or six o'clock rolls around, we can be fit to collapse into bed. But evening time in a busy household can be the most frantic time of the day. There is homework to be done, dinners to be cooked, stories to be read, dogs to be walked and bodies to be exercised. This is also the time of the day we are most likely to lose our cool, and patience can be wearing thin as fatigue and a stressful day take their toll.

With RAW, we find a quiet place to meditate after the bulk of the day is done but before all that evening activity kicks in. As a parent, the evening can be the most challenging or frustrating part of the day. When we work outside the home, we are conscious of making the most of the precious time we have at the end of the day with the people we love. If we are feeling the effects of stress or tiredness, however, we can also feel like all we want to do is flop down on the couch and lose ourselves in Netflix. The tug-of-war that emerges from these two states can often lead to snarky exchanges, irritability or rows, which are usually followed by pangs of shame or guilt. If we work at home, we can feel short-changed if we're not getting any kind of break in the evening, as the chores never seem to end. This can have the same results, and we often end up bringing a not-so-wonderful version of ourselves to the dinner table.

This is where the second meditation of the day comes in. This evening practice allows our nervous systems to reboot before we move into the next phase of our day. It's another opportunity for us to switch off that inner alarm that may still be ringing from earlier stresses. By sitting down to experience a few moments of stillness and silence before the evening events kick off, we give strength and energy to the parts of our brain that will promote calmness, patience and kindness around the people we love the most, while turning the volume down on all the parts that are making us feel uneasy. We emerge then from our evening meditation as a version of ourselves that is far more capable and willing to enjoy everyone's company without losing the head.

For me, one of the unexpected benefits of the second meditation of the day was the extra energy I had. I seemed to have far more than usual, particularly around my children's bedtime, which I discussed earlier. It makes sense, though, that I would have more energy because the internal guilt-war wasn't hoovering it all up. Being pulled in different directions emotionally is exhausting, as is staying in a mode where the stress response is always firing. Once we flick that switch, we are free to enjoy our time and the people close to us without the added distractions. Our parasympathetic nervous system has kicked in and everything feels easier. And there's less chance of you flinging a boiled potato in anger.

With the growing worldwide trend of working from home, the evening meditation has never held such importance. In my work with companies across Ireland, a major issue for employees is switching off from the working day and staving off that 'work mode' into the evening. For many people who now find themselves removed from the office and at home all day, the natural breaks and punctuation points have all but disappeared: the short walks around the office, trips to the coffee machine with a chat along the way, banter about the match or the TV show, the stroll, cycle or drive home, the podcast listen on the commute. All these things can seem innocuous, but they act as natural breakers in the working day, dividers between periods of work and intense concentration. People, without necessarily realising it, were using them to switch off that stress response and give their minds and bodies a chance to reset and reserve energy. When working from home, these organic punctuation points are being removed and so too are the opportunities to detach and unwind throughout the day. So it's up to us to put new ones in, and the afternoon or evening meditation can be the perfect solution for a calmer, more patient you.

Some ancient Ayurvedic texts recommend between 5 and 7 p.m. as the best time for your evening meditation. Ayurveda is a 5,000-year-old Hindu healing system that has had an enormous influence on meditation and health practices in large parts of the world. These were developed, however, when life was a little simpler and 24-hour super-markets and gyms weren't a thing and people didn't watch *Game of Thrones* or play *Fortnite* until four in the morning. So finding a time that works for you is the most important thing. Remember, we don't have to seek enlightenment – we just want to splash a bit of cold water on our amygdala and come at the rest of our day with a cooler, less reactive, more optimistic mind.

My advice on the second meditation of the day is to lock in the morning meditation first. When you feel that is almost second nature, then you can think about introducing the evening meditation. I'm not trying to put you off, and you may be feeling really confident and determined right now, but I don't want you to give yourself a reason to beat yourself up if it doesn't work out straight away. This whole process of establishing a meditation practice that really works for you is about self-kindness and doing what you can manage without taking on too much too soon. There's no rush, and it's far more important that your meditation seat is somewhere you want to come back to without feeling that you should be doing more.

BE FLEXIBLE

The guidelines I'm giving you for your practice are just that – guidelines. We're all different and our schedules are different. Some people work nights; some don't work at all. Some of us need that meditation time in the dark of the morning; others need that time to sleep, exercise, jump in the sea or, like one friend of mine, do her laundry. Meditation will only work if it fits snugly into your day without causing more hassle, so find a system and a time that works for you. I have friends who much prefer to sit in silence after the kids and partner have been packed off to school. My mate Dave does his morning meditation in his car before work. Some parents like to wait until Baba is having a nap, and others take their meditation on a walk, mindfully listening and breathing as they go. It's really important to know that you can't do this wrong! No one is a better judge of how well your meditation practice is working for you than you. Try out different ways, and see what fits in seamlessly and what feels jarring or awkward. All I ask is that you keep turning up.

You may find five 16-second meditations across the day is perfect for you. Spending a half hour in your favourite armchair before the little ones wake up could be your perfect sweet spot. Hell, I even meditate in the toilets at work! The length of an ad break and one song allows me enough time to breathe my way to being a more present, tuned-in radio presenter. Sometimes I just don't feel that funny, and I know a few moments of connection will open that creative tap and help me to tune in to some unfiltered inspiration, even if those moments are found in the jacks. As your relationship with meditation continues to grow, your perception of waiting will be completely transformed. Airport queues, supermarket lines, train stations and bus stops will all become free opportunities to get your calm on. Even a short trip in a lift is a challenge to see how many mindful breaths I can fit in.

It's a bit like owning a dog. Before we got Buddy, Corrina and I wondered how we were going to fit him in around all the stuff we do during the day. How was he not going to be a giant pain the backside as we attempted to navigate already cluttered days? But as any dog owner knows, once they arrive, they just kind of slot in. And, boy, are they worth it. Instead of asking how you'd cope with a dog in your life, you start to wonder how you ever managed without them, and it even seems hard to remember the house without them. They offer an intangible improvement to the general well-being of the household that benefits everyone. When you allow taking time out to breathe to fit into your day in a manner that works for you, it becomes like the family dog, where you can't remember what life was like without it. What's more, you won't want to go back to the way it was before.

GIVE YOURSELF A BREAK

Life is unpredictable. Just ask Tiger Woods. Things change, we change, shit happens. You may just be getting your meditation practice off to a good start when your work hours change, your relationship dissolves or you have a health challenge that knocks you sideways. Maybe you just get caught up with … stuff. It's fine! It happens to us all. If you forget to meditate, just start again the next day. It's not a race, you're not going to lose 'enlightenment points' and you won't lose your meditation licence. Just be kind to yourself. This is probably the most important tip I will give you because it's where most people tend to fall down.

Chances are, one of the reasons you're reading this book is because you're aware on some level that you criticise yourself with your thoughts. That inner voice is chipping away at you, and the perfectionist aspect of your personality never seems satisfied. Meditation makes us kinder to ourselves and turns the volume down on that critical inner voice. But, sometimes, before our practice has a chance to get off the ground, we berate ourselves for forgetting a session, not 'doing it properly', having thoughts, feeling awkward or getting distracted. Phrases like 'typical me' or 'I can't even breathe right' run through our heads and suddenly it all feels like a big chore. Pretty soon, 'failing' at meditation has become another big stick with which to beat ourselves over the head, and we don't feel worthy or deserving enough to keep it going. And so we stop.

Meditation is a wonderful opportunity to become aware of those critical inner thoughts that force us off track from time to time. It's a chance for us to practise daily replacing those thoughts with kind, supportive ones, reminding ourselves that this is a new process, it takes time, we don't have to be perfect. Pretty soon, those kinder thoughts will become a habit in themselves and filter into the other parts of our day where we may also be hypercritical of our behaviour. Because there is nothing to be cross with ourselves about. You can't get meditation wrong. There is no way to 'fail'. As Yoda so beautifully put it in *The Empire*

Strikes Back, 'Try not. Do. Or do not. There is no try.' Just keep turning up and it will happen. You may not be able to levitate an X-wing out of a Dagobah swamp, but you will find more peace and joy.

BE PATIENT

'Shouldn't I be seeing colours or something?' A lot of the time, people ask me about what they should be experiencing when meditating. There's a Zen Buddhist concept called 'beginner's mind' or *Shoshin*.[25] The idea is that you drop all preconceptions and approach whatever you are doing with an attitude of openness. How many times have you gone into a conversation expecting a particular outcome and it goes another way? Or maybe you've fallen out of love with your job because, when you wake in the morning, you feel you already know how the workday will go? Adopting a touch of *Shoshin* can put some distance between our preconceptions and what actually transpires, just enough space to make room for surprises.

When it comes to meditation, beginner's mind is exactly where we want to be. It involves treating every meditation as your first, carrying no expectation of what's supposed to occur and just experiencing it as it happens, one breath at a time. There is no path of meditation milestones that you're supposed to hit along the way. There are no coloured belts or weight classes. After six months of sitting with your eyes closed, you don't just suddenly start seeing interdimensional gateways and the faces of Hindu gods. What you experience is entirely up to you. Imagine it as if every time you close your eyes in meditation you're exploring your own individual garden. There are sunny parts, dark parts and places in the weeds that haven't been looked at in years. Each person's garden is different, and what happens in your neighbour's has no connection to yours.

Some people have far-out experiences on a meditation cushion. They see colours or strange places, feel a divine presence or have life-changing eureka moments of realisation. For most of us, however, the experience is less intergalactic space rocket and more a nice Sunday drive with your granny, where you stop for ice cream and pet a donkey. I'm not sure about that last analogy but you get my point. Having that beginner's mind and lowering your expectations of what might happen when you meditate will help you settle into it a bit easier. If something weird and wonderful happens, that's great, but try not to get caught up in the expectation of it happening again or become disappointed if it doesn't.

It's not uncommon to feel waves of emotion when we are still and quiet. We can experience a lovely blissful state and might start smiling for no particular reason. Sometimes, there are waves of sadness, anger or love or just plain boredom. Whether the emotions you feel are negative or positive, try not to attach any importance to them or become concerned about why you're experiencing them. You're simply dipping your toe in the stream of consciousness at that particular moment and witnessing the push and pull of whatever currents happen to be passing through.

For the most part, though, meditation is like a tennis match where the ball of your awareness bounces between the focus of your attention, like your breath or a mantra, and whatever random thoughts come by to say hello. When we realise our mind has wandered, the ball bounces back to our meditation. People come to me all the time saying things like, 'Other people can do this but I don't think meditation is for me. My mind is jumping all over the place. There must be something wrong with me!' There's nothing wrong with you if that happens. In fact, there's something right with you. Having thoughts means you're alive! The minute they disappear, it's game over. Remember, you're going to have thoughts. We have up to 80,000 of them a day and they are not going anywhere. Your mind will wander, that's a guarantee. If your mind wanders all over the place like a drunk ould fella on the way home from the pub, that doesn't mean you're doing it wrong.

The great news is that science shows there are powerful moments of change in each moment of mind-wandering. Remember the physical changes in the brain brought on by regular meditation that we spoke about earlier? Well, the same research has shown that some of those changes occur in the very part of the brain responsible for mind-wandering. So instead of despairing that there's something wrong with you because you keep having thoughts, celebrate the fact that the more you meditate, the less your brain will wander in the future.

ENJOY IT, STAY HUMBLE AND THERE'S NO NEED TO TELL EVERYBODY

When I was twelve I went to piano lessons. My mother would drop me off at an old Victorian house on O'Connell Avenue in Limerick and in I would go. I still remember the smell of the leather satchel that my piano notes were kept in. I'm not entirely sure why I was using a bag that is making this paragraph sound like a Dickens novel. I mean, I had plenty of Manchester United bags at home that would have done fine. Maybe my mother felt playing the piano deserved a bag of considerable elegance. Anyway, the teacher was an old man. I say old but he was probably 50 – ancient to a 12-year-old. He had a good reputation, apparently, and my mother seemed to think he was worthy of my raw talent.

What she didn't know, however, was that he had two pianos for teaching – one in the 'good room' at the front of the house and one in the back room. Each week he would double-book the lesson and have his prize student in the front room and me out the back. I remember listening to the confident sounds coming from the other room as I did my best to hammer out 'Mary Had a Little Lamb' on my piano, which was riddled with broken keys. Now, 'Mary Had a Little Lamb' is not the most interesting of tunes at the best of times. It only has three notes – C, D and E. But when you're trying to play it and the D doesn't work at all, it loses even more charm. It was as if I was playing the tune but with a really bad signal so it kept breaking up at certain parts. The teacher never came near me for the hour so I just continued to bash out two-thirds of the greatest shepherd-based tune ever written. Of course, not knowing any better, I thought this was how all piano lessons were conducted and presumed that, someday, if I worked hard enough, I would be promoted to a full working piano in a room that didn't have stuffed dead animals and a smell of old overcoats.

When my mother picked me up she'd ask me how it went and I'd say 'fine', just relieved that it was all over and I could fling the cursed satchel into the wardrobe for another week. At some point, I can't remember how, my mother eventually realised that this guy was taking the absolute piss and read him the riot act. I was then moved to the Limerick School of Music where I was able to learn proper classical pieces from a proper teacher. I must say, I took to the piano like a duck to pasta and quit six months later.

How does all this tie into meditation, I hear you ask?

Well, I want you to enjoy meditation. I know you can reach a point where you will look forward to doing it every day. It can become your lovely oasis of calm and reassurance as you settle into the comforting groove of spending precious time with yourself. I don't want it to become a piano lesson. I don't want you to feel like it's a chore, that you have to practise or you'll get in trouble or feel guilty every time you see one of my posts on Instagram.

The thing is, I was actually very good at the piano. When I wasn't playing a broken piano beside a stuffed stoat, I was working out my favourite pop tunes on the piano at home. I was making up my own songs and experimenting with chords and note progressions, something I still love to do today. But the way I was learning wasn't for me. Broken pianos aside, classical tunes did nothing for me and I felt sick every time I had to go for another lesson. It was a drag. If you're forcing yourself to follow a style of meditation that doesn't work for you, it will also become a drag. You won't look forward to it and you won't keep it up. So experiment. Try stuff out. See what works and what doesn't work.

Some folk love to pick a style or particular meditation and stick with it until it becomes part of them. Others like to keep it loose and do whatever suits them at that particular moment. Personally, I use all the meditations I've outlined in the last chapter. If I'm feeling really buzzy and stressed, I'll do a body scan. If I'm worried about something, I'll use the 'I trust' mantra. If I'm concerned for someone else or the world, I'll use a loving-kindness meditation. If I want a quick fix of calm in a stressful moment, I'll use the 16-second meditation. I like to keep it fluid. Yesterday, I was in a beautiful forest so I let a walking meditation be my second session of the day. Sometimes it's nice to open one of the apps like Insight Timer and do a kind of lucky dip and let the app decide what you need right then.

John Kabat-Zinn, founder of the pivotal Mindfulness Based Stress Reduction technique, or MBSR, says in his enlightening book *Wherever You Go There You Are: Mindfulness Meditation for Everyday Life*, 'There is really and truly no one "right way" to practise. It is best to encounter each moment with freshness. We look deeply into it, and then we let go into the next moment, not holding on to the last one.'[26] Play your personal instrument of peace whatever way you want, as long as it means you keep turning up. Just don't play 'Mary Had a Little Lamb', OK?

CHAPTER 11

THE EXCUSE MONSTER IS REAL!

Your mind is an excuse factory. It has the ability to come up with endless reasons why sitting in silence for five minutes is just not possible right now. Like when I ask one of my kids to empty the dishwasher, an avalanche of excuses comes tumbling out and it seems like the world's greatest ordeal. Our minds are trained to be frantic, agitated and unmercifully busy, and they don't like to be interrupted from their runaway train of thought. So when we attempt to do something like meditation, where our world of distraction and noise is being threatened, then the excuse factory swings into action with a conveyor belt of reasons not to meditate. So here are my top five favourite excuses and the reasons why you should, when you hear yourself say them, put your fingers in your ears and go 'la la la!'

I DON'T HAVE THE TIME

'If you don't have time to meditate for 20 minutes a day, then you should meditate for 40 minutes a day'. – Zen proverb

A real doozie and by far the most popular. Yesterday I spent 40 minutes on Amazon looking at weighted blankets. This is not time I will get back. We spend so much of our time on screens, mindlessly scrolling and clicking, and never question for a minute that it may be a complete waste of our time. Suddenly, when we suggest that we might take five minutes to breathe in silence, it seems like a preposterous proposal that someone of our acute busyness and importance would not have an iota of time for, even if it is proven to benefit us in a myriad of ways. How often do we hit Snooze, scroll Instagram or knowingly allow the 'Next Episode' feature on Netflix to kick in as we lie helpless on the couch? We are not the oh-so efficient time auditors that we credit ourselves to be. We are not bent over the spreadsheets counting minutes in and seconds out. We treat our time like we eat garlic-and-cheese fries after six pints – with little care and even less attention.

Which is fine, by the way. No one needs to be panicking about wasting a nanosecond here and there. But don't tell me you haven't got time for a 16-second meditation, because it's just not true. Can you *really* not set your alarm clock for five minutes earlier? Can you *really* not ask your partner to keep an eye on the potatoes for few moments while you shrink your amygdala? The truth is we make time for whatever we feel is really important to us. So if you feel you can't make time for a few minutes of self-care that is proven to make you happier, calmer and less stressed, then what are you making time for? We make time to brush our teeth in the morning, to clean our bodies and iron our shirts. Isn't how we want to feel for the rest of the day as important as our mouthwash?

This is why routine is so important, as discussed in the previous chapter. Making your meditation part of your regular routine shuts up your excuse monster before it has a chance to open its mouth. Make it a non-negotiable. Put it in your diary. Set an alarm or a reminder. If between 10 and 10.15 a.m. is your only chance in the day to do your meditation, then protect that time at all costs! Tell your friend you'll meet them at 10.30; put your phone on Do Not Disturb; tell the man from the gas company to call back later. The more you prioritise this time for yourself and guard it from being bumped out for something less important, the more it will weave itself into the fabric of your day and it will be as normal as putting out the bins or washing your hair. The amazing thing is that when we meditate regularly it actually feels like we have *more* time. As meditation helps us to become more focused, present and energetic, we tend to spend less time on things that are not important and more time on the good stuff. Suddenly, our days open up for all the things that actually matter to us and we are less likely to hear ourselves say 'I don't have the time.'

There is also the temptation to put off meditating until a time when you are less busy, when you don't have as many things on your plate. This is precisely the time to lean into meditation. The fact that you think your life is so busy that you couldn't fit five minutes in it for yourself means that you are lacking clarity on your priorities. It's a sign that your balance is off, and beginning a meditation practice is just the thing to bring some focus on where you should be placing your energy. It may feel the opposite but, believe me, it's during those periods when I'm at my craziest that I know I need to make more time for sitting in silence. So much of our resistance around making small positive changes is down to our conditioning and all the habits and influences we've picked up along the way. But at the bottom of all of these reasons not to listen to that lethargic voice in your head is a simple but exceptionally important argument for making time to sit down in peace and silence – YOU DESERVE IT!

I'M TOO TIRED

I know this one. It's a classic. What we're really saying to ourselves when we come out with this gem is, 'I'm too tired to sit in a chair.' Hilarious! As I've mentioned before, we are creatures of habit and our general way of dealing with fatigue, either mental or physical, is to detach and distract. Flopping onto the couch, losing ourselves in a box set, plugging into the PlayStation or dissolving into the iPad are our usual responses to feeling lethargic and weary. And that's all they are, a habit, and it's one we can get out of. Do we ever feel more rested or more energised after doing any of those things? Not really, because they mostly just use up mental energy we said we didn't have in the first place. Most importantly, though, if you are feeling 'too tired', meditation could be just what you need.

New research from Oregon State University has shown that entrepreneurs who regularly practise mindfulness meditation report lower levels of exhaustion. According to the author of the study, Charles Murnieks from OSU's College of Business, 'As little as 70 minutes a week, or 10 minutes a day, of mindfulness practice may have the same benefits as an extra 44 minutes of sleep a night.'[27] Good news, right? Who doesn't want more sleep? So next time you hear yourself say you're too tired to meditate, know that what you're actually saying is 'I'm too tired to feel less tired!'

IT'S TOO HARD – MY MIND IS JUST TOO BUSY

A lot of this fear that your mind is broken stems from the misconception that you are expected to clear your mind of all thought. It's as if we somehow had the capacity to hit Factory Reset on our brains and wipe all thoughts from it. As I've said, you need your thoughts, they're keeping you alive, and they're not going anywhere. In fact, don't we need them for the act of meditation itself? Think about it. Isn't it a thought that lets you know your mind has wandered? Isn't it a thought that brings your focus back to your breath? We're not trying to remove our thoughts or banish them for being bold – we are simply trying to become more aware of the kinds of thoughts we're spending time with and learning to not let them rule everything we do. By straining or forcing ourselves not to have thoughts, we can actually give more power to them. It's a bit like trying really hard to empty a jar of bees. The harder we try the angrier they get! It's easier to let them fly out of their own accord.

People often feel that meditation itself makes their minds more frantic. I really believe that our minds don't get any busier when we sit down in silence – it's just that, by quietening down for a few moments and removing distractions, we become aware of just how busy they always are. Like turning on a light in a messy attic, we suddenly get a glimpse of how crazy it all is up there. Of course your mind is going to feel like it's jumping all over the place in the beginning. But, gradually, as you get used to spending time with your thoughts, they will start to feel less frantic and disruptive. Meditation helps us to sort out our mental attic and, bit by bit, we bring order to the chaos. Before we know it, there's way more space for the things that are important to us – besides, that is, the Christmas and Halloween decorations and that abs-workout contraption you haven't used in 15 years.

I TRIED MEDITATION BUT IT'S TOO BORING

This brings us back to our expectation of what will happen when we meditate. We live in a culture of instant gratification, and some people don't find meditation stimulating enough. If you go into meditation expecting the mental equivalent of a St Patrick's Day parade then you may be left feeling disappointed and the experience may feel a bit boring. If, however, you can see it as a break from all the stimulation we are exposed to from the minute we wake to the moment we put our head on the pillow, then you will begin to relish every simple moment with your breath, with your mantra, with yourself. Dr Fadel Zeidan, from the UCSD Center for Mindfulness in California, says, 'Don't expect to experience bliss. Don't even expect to feel better. Just say, "I'm going to dedicate the next 5 to 20 minutes to meditation."' By expecting less, we get more from the experience.

There is a chance, however, that you are determined to get some kind of tangible pleasure from meditation and are currently banging the desk with your fist, like a police sergeant in an 80s action movie, and screaming, 'Godammit, Whelan, I need to see results and I need to see 'em now!' In that case, Sarge, let's talk dopamine. Dopamine is the pleasure chemical that is released in the brain when we engage in something enjoyable like sex, eating yummy food, listening to our favourite song or seeing Munster beat Leinster. (I don't get much dopamine these days!) It's our own, brain-produced opioid that lets us know that what we're doing is a pleasurable activity. The problem with this much sought-after chemical, however, is that it tends not to last, and we can develop a tolerance for it if we keep engaging in the same activities. It's the same reason that addicts need to up their dosage of their chosen substance or behaviour in order to continue to get the same high.

Meditation also promotes the release of dopamine. In fact, studies have shown that advanced practitioners can experience a boost in dopamine production of up to 65 per cent![28] But here's the thing: the dopamine produced by meditation does not suffer the same down-regulation of pleasure we get from other things like music, money, sex and drugs, nicotine and alcohol. In her 2013 study, neurophysiologist Patricia Sharp and her team at BGSU Ohio found that the dopamine produced by meditation doesn't diminish the more we access it. On the contrary, it appears to increase the more you meditate.[29] In other words, not only does the pleasure we get from learning to meditate increase over time, the novelty never wears off! So if the idea of meditation seems too boring to take on board, just remember that it's the most efficient, best value for money, most pleasure-inducing drug around, and you don't have to go to a scary man down an alley to get it – it's free! How's that for results, Sarge?

I'M NOT IN THE MOOD

Popular online meditation advocate Waylon Lewis puts it nicely: 'The point of meditation isn't to be peaceful, to be better than where you are now or to get away from everything. It's to be present, present with whatever is.' Some days we're in great form, feeling like we're high-fiving the world. Other days we want to stick pencils in people's eyes. Our moods are predictable in their unpredictability, and anything can sway us one way or the other.

Meditation isn't a fair-weather pastime that we only reach for when we're feeling chipper. It's a boat we sit in every day, no matter what our internal sea is doing. There will be days when you're angry or pissed off and sitting in silence feels like the last thing you want to do. Ranting and raving is probably what you'd choose off the menu, if you could. You might be feeling what my sister likes to call 'plop', where the only thing you feel like doing is eating a packet of Jammie Dodgers from both ends at the same time. Maybe you're sad, depressed, anxious or fearful. When we meditate, we're not trying to devalue or trivialise emotions we may be feeling in that particular moment. In fact, it's the opposite. We want to bring them to the table and let them have their say. By sitting with our emotions, no matter how negative they may be, we honour them, give them space to come out and, more often than not, their power over us diminishes in the process.

It's so important that we feel what we gotta feel. Nobody wants to be that person who paints on the smile and pretends that everything is hunky-dory when it's clearly not. Meditation can move us away from our habitual practice of attempting to supress, numb, cover up or distract from how we're really feeling. Giving the emotions a chance to be felt can often defuse them. You may stand up from your meditation, however, and feel just as annoyed as when you sat down. And that's fine too. Stormy seas or tranquil lake, we put the boat in the water and see what happens.

Of course, it's not just negative moods that can cause us to drop our practice like a hot snot. Sometimes we can get so cocky that we're such happy, Zen, balanced meditation wizards, we forget to do the one thing that got us to that place in the first instance. This certainly happened to me, and I presumed just telling everyone about how great meditation was would get me through the week, skipping around like a *Winning Streak* contestant on happy pills. My practice fell to the wayside and the stresses and anxieties of daily life began to weigh me down again. That determination you had at the start can fade and you take our foot off the gas. A midweek bottle of wine means the morning meditation is sacrificed for sleep. You say you'll meditate on the train but end up driving. You need to send an important morning email and promise yourself you'll get around to meditating later. The dog needs a walk so you'll do an extra-long one at bedtime. Before you know it, you've sacrificed the precious few minutes you had fought hard to allocate for yourself and, pretty soon, you're back to doing everything for that particular group of people, which always seems to float back in and take up all our time – EVERYBODY ELSE!

You can't get nourishing, healing, energising time for yourself if you don't make the time. You're reading this book because you know, at some level, that you deserve to feel more like yourself. You deserve not to be caught up in a cycle of reacting and over-reacting. You deserve to feel less stressed out and more tuned in. Remember the science – the positive benefits of meditation only really come when we do it every day. If we forget once or twice or life gets in the way, that's fine! Just start again and don't beat yourself up. And when you're meditating like a total boss and #LivingYourBestLife, remember to stay humble and, you've guessed it, just keep turning up!

At this point, I hope you're mildly convinced that there's something in, as my friend calls it, 'all that breathing stuff'. If, however, you're still on the fence and thinking of swapping it all for a good bottle of Merlot, hang in there. There are still some stress-busting tips I want to bring your way and it involves the title of a song that my wife happens to love.

CHAPTER 12

IT'S ALL ABOUT THAT BASS

Outside of purposely sitting down to meditate, opportunities to connect with our purest selves are available to us all the time. I've mentioned Dave, my old mate and radio co-host already. He is a musician. Like, a proper musician. He studied music in college and played in heavy metal bands with names that involved devils and sacrifice. And he's very annoying. He's the musical equivalent of those guys in school who could just try a sport for the first time and be good at it. Dave can pick up an instrument and instantly play it at a competent level. At one point, he decided that the bass guitar deserved his attention so he set about learning a few tunes. Now, if it was you or me, we would probably start with, I don't know, a certain classic about a girl who owned some very insecure lambs? No, Dave, jumped right in with absolute bass boss, Sting. Sting plays in time signatures so weird, Q from *Star Trek: TNG* would have difficulty keeping up (#amirite, fellow trekkies?). But Dave just seems able to lock into a groove and pretty soon he has lost all track of time as he plays away for hours. I asked him to put into his own words how he felt when he played the bass:

'I've been a guitar player since I was 12. It's such a source of joy for me. When I began my career as a producer, I needed a bass to get sounds synths couldn't match. I got a cheap Squier Jazz Bass and my life changed. Before I ever knew what meditating was, I would tell people about losing hours and hours to bass playing. Slowly, I began realising it did more for me than just playing the instrument. I felt calmer after it. I felt happier. I felt like I needed to do it. In a good way. Then, I started to improve the ingredients. Got a better bass. Got something that allowed me to play with headphones. Turned off the lights. Built a cushion bed on the floor. Plonked myself down and played. For hours. And now I do that at least once a week. Put the kids to bed. Start at 9 p.m. Usually head to bed around midnight. Three hours. I don't think of the notes. I just play. That's the difference between guitar and bass for me. Guitar demands my active brain. Bass switches that part off. Having fallen in love with meditation over the past five years, I quickly realised it has the same effect on me as bass playing. I meditate daily. I play bass weekly. It's like a super-meditation session. Would I feel like I was missing something if I skipped a daily meditation?

Sure but no big deal. A week without a bass session would feel way more like a hole for me.'

I love that, for Dave, playing the bass became more than just a hobby or a skill. It became a destination where time seems to dissolve and some kind of healing happens. It's like he's sliding his brain into neutral so that the revs can drop and he can freewheel into a space where he's connected to something more personal and uplifting. These moments are so special, moments where we lose track of time and delve into the deeper parts of our experience, where everything seems to flow from a place of lightness and connection. This is the power of play. It's mindfulness in action, pulling us into the present moment so we're not worried about the future or ruminating on the past.

Whether you play an instrument or not, finding moments of play in your day can be a hugely powerful tool to create more peace and joy in your life. When we're kids, we do it naturally all the time. You may have seen it with your own children. They'll disappear into their bedrooms and get lost in a game or an imagined scenario. They are totally immersed in it. You may have a toy you remember spending all those moments with, totally engrossed and lost in the play. As I mentioned before, for me, it was Action Man – that eagle-eyed, fuzzy-haired soldier figure I absolutely loved. I had all the paraphernalia: motorbike and sidecar, transport truck, tank, assault tower and a helicopter that had 'incredible rotor action' until the batteries leaked inside and it never worked again.

Action Man and I were best buddies – I loved everything about him, and I didn't even mind when his curled-up rubber fingers kept getting stuck in the sleeve of his uniform. In fairness, I think he was a terrible soldier, as he showed absolutely no loyalty to king or country. All his accessories were from different armies and eras, which meant that one minute he was an SAS scuba operative and the next he was a member of the French Foreign Legion. But he never backed away from a battle, most of which took place in the shrubbery in my back garden. Like real-life soldiers, his eyes were controlled by a lever in the back of his skull, and my favourite thing to do was attach a zip line to the banister and let him fly down and kick another Action Man in the back of the head. I remember so clearly that, one time, he flew down the zip wire, kicked his enemy in the head and then flipped into the jeep and landed in the perfect driving position. It was absolutely epic and no one was there to see it. But it happened!

Action Man was my mindfulness tool long before I had any concept of what that was. Like all children, I didn't need to be told how to connect with my own sense of flow; how to direct myself into the present moment. I had an innate ability to find moments of mindfulness throughout my day. Action Man and I just headed off on another adventure, and time and all its limits and constraints simply disappeared until the battle was won or my dinner was ready.

I bet you're thinking about your favourite toy right now. Remember those wonderful places you'd wander off to in your imagination? I see my daughter, Rosie, go to those same places for hours in her bedroom, dressing up as a genie or, her particular favourite, pretending to be a wolf. Somewhere along the way, however, we forget to play and those timeless moments disappear from our day. We are caught up in 'stuff', and that precious skill to effortlessly find the present moment is lost. We get into the habit of making room for all the things we feel we should do, and the things we'd like to do are pushed out. It's a startling moment when someone asks you 'What do you do for fun?' and you can't answer them!

If this is resonating with you, the purpose of all this is not to make you feel bad. It's just to let you know that there is a whole other way of finding peace in your mind and in your day that you actually know about already. Play! You trained in it for years as a child. You're already an expert. It's just a matter of rekindling that flame and bringing that part of yourself back to life. If someone I know is struggling with sitting by themselves, finding meditation hard or too intense or boring, I remind them of play and tell them to start there. We always had the skill to sit and be with ourselves – we were born with it – but we just got distracted along the way.

If you feel like you've lost touch with that playful part of you and everything seems a bit serious, ask yourself this question: is there something enjoyable that I used to do where I lost track of time? This doesn't necessarily have to be a game or a sport. This could be a hobby or a craft. Maybe it was simply walking by yourself or reading a book. Not finding anything? Try widening the circle. Is there anything that you used to do *with someone else* where you had fun and lost track of time. Keep it clean now ... Perhaps you did jigsaws with your mum, played with your pet, sat in a tree with your best friend. Whatever comes to mind, no matter how silly or pointless it might feel, try to go there in your mind. What did it feel like in your body when you did it? Did you feel relaxed, excited, passionate, skilful? Did you laugh or feel confident, calm or in control? What part of it brought you the most pleasure and why?

When it was no longer acceptable to play with Action Man in public, I used to love five-a-side soccer, and now I really miss it. But when I think about what I actually enjoyed about it, sure the football was fun, but the real enjoyment came from the banter with the lads before and after – the slagging, the laughing, the catching up on what I'd missed and the planning of what was to come. A funny conversation after the match, leaning on my car for a few minutes, could be more enjoyable than the whole game!

Tapping into our playful nature can be incredibly beneficial in all areas of our lives. It allows us to be more creative,
to find more joy, to better enjoy our work and to approach
everything with a greater sense of ease. And in a challenging
world there are even more reasons to allow ourselves to play
a bit more. Recent scientific studies suggest that how we perceive and handle stress can be greatly affected by how play-
fully we approach life. A 2013 study from the University of
Illinois focused on a large group of university students and
found that students who exhibited even a moderate amount
of playfulness experienced less stress and had better coping
mechanisms for dealing with perceived stress when it arose.[30]
Interestingly, they also found that more playful individuals
were less inclined to turn to coping mechanisms that tend to
internalise stress, like self-blame, and were also less likely to
try to avoid or escape stress. Instead, they were more likely
to 'attack stressors directly'. In other words, they were less
critical of themselves under pressure and took more deci-
sive action on facing obstacles. So, it could be said, having
a playful approach to everything we do not only means we
experience less stress but we are more likely to be able to
cope with it, if and when it arises. And when the you-know-
what hits the fan, those who practise playfulness are less
likely to beat themselves up over it.

So how do we begin to put this playfulness into action
in our everyday lives then? Let me introduce you to the

embarrassing dad skateboard …

I have a memory of being about 10 and in a skate shop with my parents. They were asking me if I wanted a skateboard and, for some reason, I was undecided and taking ages to make up my mind. Eventually, I heard, 'Look, do you want the skateboard or not?' 'No,' I whimpered and we all left. I have no idea why that moment stuck in my memory files but for some reason it did. So, fast forward 30-odd years and I'm in a skate shop again. This time, though, I'm the parent and I'm with my 11-year-old son, Matthew. He's picking out a board and the shop assistant is talking us through the various options of wheels and colours and trucks and styles. And that old memory comes back. And it stays with me and lingers for the next week until I find myself back in the shop again. This time, I'm shopping for me. I've always loved the look of skateboards. They're such an iconic, simple design and, even if you never rode one, they're really nice to look at. Kind of like a 99 ice cream or a brand-new leather football, they just look so pleasant and you want to touch them. So, this time, I won't say no. I'm in charge and I'm not leaving with a whimper.

The young woman selling it is unmercifully cool, with strands of different colours in her blond hair and piercings and baggy clothes. I enquire if many dads come in to buy boards and she says yes but I'm not sure if she actually approves of that kind of behaviour. She answers all my basic, beginner, parent-y questions with a perfect blend of retail politeness and impressive indifference. Eventually, I choose my board, which is a cruiser type, slightly bigger than a normal trick board, smaller than a longboard. I ask her does she think I should buy a helmet and pads. 'Definitely,' she replies with a worrying level of certainty. I buy all my bits and head off with the board tucked under my arm, feeling like one of those cool skateboard guys from the telly, when, in reality, I probably just looked like I was holding it for my son.

A week later, the Covid lockdown kicked off and everything got really weird. Dublin's bustling streets turned deserted and eerie and my office was a sea of empty desks. The weirdest part of the lockdown experience for me was not the lack of people on the streets or cars on the road: it was the absence of sound. It was *so* quiet. There wasn't even a background hum of traffic in the city centre. All you could hear were birds singing and the ventilation fans from empty office blocks. I know a lot people who found the change in the city extremely hard to deal with. Every time we stepped out of our front doors, we were reminded of just how different everything was. It could make us anxious, fearful and unsettled and, for many, this new situation revealed a hidden and unexpected comfort in the usual noise and clamour of a busy Irish street. It was only when the volume on the daily racket was turned down that so many people began to miss it for what it unknowingly offered us – a sense that everything was normal and OK.

For those of you who are lucky to work in the countryside or a less hectic environment, the change mightn't have been so dramatic. But for those of us who spend our entire working week in the centre of all the madness, it was a gear shift that many found hard to handle. Some couldn't bear to be in town because it just didn't feel right. I think I would have been the same if it weren't for one thing – the skateboard. The national weirdness coincided with this new object in my life. Deserted streets, which would normally have freaked me out, now became a giant abandoned skate park. The best thing was, there was no one around to crash into! I could learn, wobble, fall and embarrass the hell out of myself in a really safe environment. Well, as safe as any forty-year-old on wheels could be.

There's one important thing about learning to skateboard – it's mindfulness in motion. It's impossible to be worried about what might happen next week or fret about something you did last year when every ounce of your attention is focused on not falling off and breaking your neck. You can't help but be in the present moment when you're moving at speed and surrounded by concrete. And this is true for learning any new skill or hobby. It becomes all-consuming by its very nature, its newness, and it requires you to snap out of regular, predictable thought patterns so you can make room for all the new information coming in. During the pandemic, I continued to travel in and out of the radio studio as, amazingly, I was deemed an essential worker! Each day, when I left the office, I found this challenging, exciting and unpredictable space to go to in my head and body. It was utterly distracting from the constant flood of news reports and negativity washing over us each day, and I found the drive to get better at using the board gave me a weird sense of purpose at a time when there seemed little purpose to anything.

I must say, at this point, that I was one of the fortunate ones. Despite all my live stage work disappearing overnight, I still had my radio job and I still had money coming in. So many others had and still have businesses or careers that have really suffered and my heart goes out to them. For them, jumping on a skateboard right now could be low on their list of priorities. Alternatively, immersing yourself in an activity that pulls you into the present moment could be just what you need in times of crisis. If it feels right, then go for it. You alone are the best judge when the time is right to become a bit more playful.

So what exactly was happening in my brain when I was exploring my midlife crisis on wheels? What are the scientific reasons why taking on a new hobby and becoming more playful with our time and attitude can have such a positive impact on our sense of wellbeing? I caught up with my friend author and neuroscientist Dr Sabina Brennan, who is the Tony Hawk of brain function. She explained:

'Unfortunately, with modern life, we're spending pretty much all of our lives on autopilot. We're not having those moments of present-mindedness and this is why you need to keep learning. You need to keep doing new things, as they are the things that will keep you present and focused. Because the things you've been doing all your life on repeat, they can just happen. And your brain benefits from novelty and learning. It rewards you by creating new connections in your brain, richer connectivity in your brain and more brain cells. You want as many connections in your brain and as many brain cells as possible and they really just come with learning.'

The skateboarding was literally firing up my brain, creating new pathways, new connections, new memories and helping my brain to recognise more patterns, something it really likes to do. Most importantly of all, though, learning was releasing something in my brain that we humans can't get enough of – dopamine, that pleasure chemical. Each time we learn something new we release dopamine, and that keeps us coming back for more. Sabina explains:

'Dopamine gives you that sense of reward and then encourages you to seek more. That's actually why learning is rewarding. Dopamine plays a big role in learning and you get a buzz out of it and then you want to learn more because it's good for your brain to learn. Your brain is really just processing information, and the more information you can give it through learning, the better it can estimate and predict the likelihood of events happening.' Learning through play feeds our brain and releases the chemicals that make us feel happy.

As well as being a natural high, play also helps to create resilience and improves our ability to adapt to changes in our environment. This involves something called neuroplasticity:

'Neuroplasticity is just a fancy way of saying "the brain has the ability to change with learning". Why is it important? It's important because learning is adaptation. We have to adapt to our environment, even if it's as simple as you skateboarding and seeing that bump. You have to learn to adapt to that,' says Sabina. 'So, it's learning to adapt to living in a stressful environment, learning to adapt to living under lockdown or in a prison. Human beings are incredibly resilient and that ability to learn is what underlies resilience.'

In her fascinating book *100 Days to a Younger Brain*, Sabina points to something called 'brain reserve'.[31] Simply put, this can be seen as our brain's ability to stave off the damaging effects of ageing or disease. By adapting a healthier balance of purpose and play, we create more brain reserve and make ourselves more resilient against cognitive decline. Science shows that people who engage in more leisure activities, like walking for pleasure, visiting loved ones, going to the movies or doing volunteer work, have less risk of developing a disease like dementia. Interestingly, even if people with more brain reserve display the physical effects of dementia in their brain, they are less likely to experience the symptoms. As our brain begins to shrink from around the age of 30, stimulation of any kind grows in importance. Playing and enjoying leisure time, therefore, can literally keep our brains safe, even if it's just knitting a scarf or reading a magazine.

This is why playing a sport is so helpful to our brains. As well as the obvious physical health benefits of exercise, sport allows our brains to take in new information through all our senses, to boost learning and to release dopamine and other chemicals that give us a sense of purpose and stimulate our internal reward system. In fact, any hobby where you're learning something new, from playing the bass guitar to reading books about 70s punk bands (guilty!), will help you to ignite your brain and boost playfulness. And it makes sense. So many of the toys we buy young children are designed to encourage learning through play. They help them to take in new information while having fun. So why would it be any different when we're adults? We're the same people, just bigger! It makes sense that the more we can introduce a sense of play, the more easily and effortlessly we will learn new things and find more pleasure in it. But before you go quitting your job to become a professional balloon-animal entertainer, Sabina has a word of warning.

'All work and no play is not good for you but all play and no work is not good either. By "work", I mean purpose and meaning. So, having play all the time isn't going to make you feel great if you feel you've no purpose in life.'

I guess this is the reason why billionaires keep working when most of us think we'd be lying on a beach some-where after the first million. Without purpose, we lack the long-term stimulation our brains crave so much and, as a result, we don't get that learning-fuelled pleasure release that keeps us coming back for more. So, I guess I'd better keep following my radio and meditation dreams then, and leave full-time skateboarding to the professionals. Tony Hawk, your crown is safe …

Play also has another role for me. It turns the volume down on that 'shoulding' inner voice we talked about. It keeps me in the present moment and makes me far less likely to reach for the things that amplify my inner critic and give that nun on the end of the bed a voice. Me on a skateboard is the polar opposite to me with a hangover, and I know which one floats my boat these days. Seems like a good time to talk about alcohol.

CHAPTER 13

BOOZE, GLORIOUS BOOZE

I feel we need to talk about booze a bit more and give it its own special part of the book. In fairness, so many of us have spent so many hours and nights in its company, it would seem rude not to. Why am I including it? Well, because I think, for a lot of people, alcohol plays more of a role in affecting their moods than they care to admit. Also, for me, creating a healthier relationship with alcohol had a huge impact on my sense of well-being. I get asked a lot about my attitude to alcohol from people who are expressing an interest in cutting down or stopping altogether. Don't worry – I'm not about to launch into an anti-alcohol holier-than-thou rant. I would just like to bring you some insights that I learned from a grand experiment I conducted a couple of years ago.

I mentioned before that, for me, alcohol created a kind of civil war in my head. On one side was the desire to go out, have a laugh, relax and reward myself. On the other was a deep regret about how alcohol made me feel and a strong desire to be free of the need for it. After a night out, the battle would rage for days until the 'you deserve to relax' side would win out and the cycle would start all over again. I longed to be one of those people who could go out drinking and bounce back fresh and positive the next day. I was surrounded by people who swore they never got hangovers and seemed to just get on with it. Today, I'm not so sure those people are being entirely honest! So, one day, I decided I was sick of repeating the same boring argument in my head and I opened my laptop. I googled 'hypnotherapy for alcohol' and began my research. The next week I was in a hypnotherapist's office getting verrrry sleeepy. An hour later I was walking up the road to join my family for a trip to the panto, wondering if it had worked. That session launched me on my experiment to see if it was easy to stop drinking for a year and if it was worth it.

I'm not sure if the hypnosis actually worked or if the very act of going there and paying someone just reinforced my willpower and commitment. It's probably a mixture of the two. The very fact that I took the step of visiting someone for a hypnotherapy session showed that I was ready at some level to stop drinking, at least for a while. I had stopped drinking for a month many times before but I noticed that, after the month, I would often be drinking more than I had been. A year seemed like a true test of my resolve and a real chance to see what life was like, what *I* was like, without the weekly distraction of pints and hangovers. In general, I don't think I drank any more than your average Irish boozer, but it was clear that the older I got, the worse it made me feel. I had such a longing to discover the person underneath the need to repeatedly numb myself with booze. As much as it sounds like the lyric to a cheesy song, I felt as if he was calling to me. I wanted to see just what the landscape would look like where my moods weren't so topsy-turvy and I was more confident in my own skin. It was a very interesting year. Here are the top ten things I learned in my year without alcohol.

1. IT SET MY BRAIN FREE

The civil war was over. I could now get on with thinking about the things and people that actually mattered. I realised that alcohol could actually make you incredibly self-absorbed. Hangovers are, by their very nature, inward looking, and worrying about how you feel or what you've done or not done can take up a lot of your time and energy. When I was free of the hangovers and their associated guilt, I wasn't so self-obsessed and had more time and patience for other people. It was as if I had deleted an app that was forever draining my battery. Once the unnecessary distraction of the booze was taken out of the equation, life became a lot simpler. I didn't have to factor in how I was going to feel when planning my weekend with my family. We could now do things earlier because I wouldn't be wrecked or groggy. Getting the all-important lie-in on a Saturday or Sunday didn't seem to matter as much, as I had more energy and I was going to bed earlier anyway. There were fewer logistics to worry about when going out for an evening because taxis were now out of the picture as I could drive everywhere. Not drinking created fewer worrisome or fearful thoughts, which meant my brain and I were less hassled and more available for the fun stuff.

2. IT HAD A HUGE EFFECT ON MY MOOD

Professor David Nutt may have a slightly comical name but he knows everything about booze and its effect on the brain. In fact, he feels so passionately about the damage alcohol causes to our health, he was fired from his post as advisor to the British government for saying that alcohol is more dangerous than ecstasy and LSD.[32]

Controversial statements aside, his work has been key in demystifying the humble hangover and other more intense states such as 'hangxiety' or, as it's also known, the fear. And his research can explain why we often emotionally see-saw when we drink. Forgive me if this gets a tad science-y, but it really helped me to understand what was happening in my brain when I drank. I found it reassuring to know I wasn't mad and that there were real chemical reactions behind how I felt.

According to Nutt, it has a lot to do with something called GABA (gamma-Aminobutyric acid for the Scrabble enthusiasts).[33] Alcohol stimulates this amino acid, which has a calming effect on the brain – more GABA, more relaxation. As well as increasing GABA, alcohol also inhibits something called glutamate. This neurotransmitter can excite the brain and lead to feelings of anxiety. If you block it with booze, therefore, it leads to less anxious thoughts. Both these processes lead to a quietening of that critical inner voice that likes to 'should' us and make us feel inadequate. A couple of drinks in and the volume on that invisible scorekeeper is turned way down.

Your body, however, like an Irish dad and his immersion, doesn't like when you've been fiddling with the controls. So it attempts to rebalance things, and as the alcohol leaves your system, it sets about reducing the chillout-inducing GABA and boosting the anxiety fanboy glutamate. When you wake up, the happy vibes have left and, if you're like me, there's an angry nun on the end of the bed. It can take a day or two for the chemical levels in your brain to return to normal and this makes it even more tempting to dip back into the honeypot for more relief.

Obviously, when you've had a big night the effects of this chemical turmoil are pretty clear. If you're drinking smaller amounts, however, the changes in your mood can be far less dramatic, even almost imperceptible, but they're still there.

Your mood can be out of whack and you'll have no idea that it's the few 'harmless' glasses of wine or the couple of pints that are responsible. It was only when I stopped drinking completely that I found my mood stabilised long enough for me to feel like I knew myself. I was finally able to trust my moods too, as I didn't spend time wondering was it the booze or tiredness or stress or just life that was affecting me. Quitting alcohol is not a magic wand for your feelings and it doesn't make you happy all the time. It does, however, remove enough of the emotional clutter to allow you to think straighter and trust in your emotions more.

3. MY RELATIONSHIPS IMPROVED

When we're not fighting ourselves, we fight less with others. It's just a fact. When I quietened the inner battle around alcohol, I was more present for the relationships that really matter. Saturday-and-Sunday-morning Dad was now a much better version of himself. He had more patience, more energy and more enthusiasm for what the day could offer. And the reality is, no matter who you live with, coming in the door pissed at two in the morning is going to cause more arguments than not doing it. I have always had the propensity to be the last at the party and the first to look for more mischief, so once I learned to channel that sense of 'divilment' into other areas, there were fewer late nights and fewer frosty receptions the next day.

It's not just my home life that improved either. Because I was bringing a more emotionally stable version of myself to work, my work relationships improved. My long-suffering radio co-host, Dave, has witnessed all my ups and downs, groggy heads and shame-filled mornings. As a man who never drank alcohol in his life, I can only imagine what he had to deal with sometimes! He is, to this day, the most patient man I have ever met. As my drinking habits changed, however, there were fewer moments of friction between us and more laughs. Comedy tours together were less draining, as I wasn't burning the candle at both ends, and our radio relationship, both on and off air, definitely felt the benefit.

Another thing that arose around relationships was quality. When alcohol is taken out of the equation, you tend to meet up with people solely for the purpose of seeing them and enjoying their company. So often, we can arrange to meet someone in a pub and, if we're really honest with ourselves, it's not entirely clear if it's them or the promise of some creamy pints that has you sitting at the bar. In that year, I found I was meeting people because I really wanted to spend time with them, regardless of the location, and, when I did, I was far more mentally present.

4. MY FRIENDS CHANGED

When your drinking habits change, your friend habits do too. It's not that you'll suddenly start shedding pals like dog hairs on a couch. You will find, however, that some friends who were in the foreground of your life move into the background, and some friends who were out of the spotlight suddenly become centre stage. They shift around as your priorities do the same and that's perfectly natural. Some people are uncomfortable with this new, cleaner version of you and that's fine. A few may be inspired to join you, and others may avoid you, as you remind them of what they find difficult to change in themselves. The important thing is not to judge them for their reactions – they're just getting used to this new side to you.

One of the real benefits, though, of taking a break from alcohol is that you spend less time with people you don't actually care about that much. We've all been there. The night is coming to an end. You should probably go home but you fancy one for the road. So you end up chatting to someone who you wouldn't ordinarily go for a pint with, but they're there in front of you so you just go along with it. Maybe it's a function where the non-drinkers have headed off and you stay longer with the ones you think might be up for some craic. Because, let's face it, our patience for bullshit conversations goes up drastically when we drink! As soon as you start going to functions and events where you're not on the sauce, your tolerance for chit-chat drops dramatically. You'll find you only want to spend time with the people who really mean something to you, and as soon as you feel you've caught up on everything, you will head for that door.

Ireland is the home of the long goodbye, and when we drink, it gets even longer. Trying to get a drunk person to the exit is like trying to get a fiver off a Cavan man. It takes work and it takes patience! When I took that break from drinking, it really made me think about all the shite conversations I suffered through, all in the name of craic. That's time I could have been doing something more worthwhile, like sleeping!

5. MY BEHAVIOURS CHANGED

Drinking, as much as anything else, is a habit. Sometimes we do it even if we don't feel like it. I've often stood at a bar, scanning the array of drinks, knowing in my heart that I don't really want anything on offer – I'd much rather be on my couch with a cup of tea and a biscuit. So often, we drink because we're just used to doing it in certain situations. Ever open a bottle of wine at home on a Friday night, have one glass and then wonder what you're going to do with the rest of the bottle? My wife was forever perplexed by the bizarre collection of nearly full bottles of red wine I would leave around the kitchen. In reality, I didn't actually want them, but I was just in the habit of 'treating' myself, and the ritual I had embraced was opening a bottle of red and chowing down on a plate of Gubeen cheese and crackers.

After realising I didn't feel like the wine after all, I would convince myself I would use it in cooking, even though all I make is boiled eggs and cereal. I've never seen a TV chef slosh a generous helping of Bordeaux onto a bowl of Crunchy Nut cornflakes.

So much of our drinking comes from a 'that's what I always do', conditioned way of thinking. When we interrupt that pattern, we realise that there are other activities we'd rather be doing and other things we'd rather be drinking. This is all tied in to how we view our sense of reward. In our society, alcohol is associated with our desire to reward ourselves. On TV, we see the image of the hard-working businessman coming through the door after a tough day or week. He immediately reaches for the bottle of liquor and pours himself a stiff one. Or maybe it's the working gal who kicks off her office shoes and pours herself a big glass of white from the fridge. Booze is heavily intertwined with our sense of reward, and the idea of replacing it with something else can seem hugely uncomfortable. But with a little bit of clarity, the idea of celebrating little victories by lashing poison down your neck starts to seem a bit bizarre. In my experience, the greatest reward we can give ourselves is a clear head.

I've been very fortunate to win a number of National Radio Awards for my show over the years. In previous times, winning was the excuse I needed to drink every pint within a five-mile radius. I'd wake up with the fear and struggle to remember what was a very special moment in my radio career. Nowadays, my celebrations look a lot different. My favourite way to reward myself is to wake up the next day still buzzing from the night before. The feeling of winning any award is a special one and, if I'm lucky enough to experience it, I want it to last as long as possible. The next day, instead of being filled with fear and dread, is full of feelings of joy and pride in myself for achieving something special. You also come to realise that true celebration is not about the drink in your hand but the people you're with. It is a shared experience that doesn't require a drug to give it validation. Sure, there may be events that will seem torturous to you without the idea of alcohol to make them bearable. But that is more of a reflection on the boring nature of the event than your need to drink a load of alcohol. If the event is boring, just do what the sober people do and leave earlier – you've better things to be doing with your time!

Weddings are one of the things that make people feel like taking a break from alcohol is an impossible task. How am I supposed to get through the day? And they have a point! Irish weddings are weird when you begin to go to them sober. Large chunks of the day are dedicated to nothing other than standing around chatting and drinking. The food often seems like an afterthought and can take hours to emerge, by which time people have already started to engage in that most ancient of Irish arts – talking shite.

Weddings, or the like, can seem boring when you're not drinking because they *are* boring. Just ask my non-drinking pal, Dave! But so many people who are trying not to drink think *they're* boring rather than the event they're attending. Once you've chatted to all the people who are important to you, there's very little else to do. It's OK to leave or, at the very least, take a break.

The best wedding I've attended without partaking in alcohol was my niece's big day last year. She had organised music in the afternoon on both days. I've never danced so much in my life! I was just so glad of something to do that I got stuck in and had a whale of a time, while everyone else stood around drinking and ignoring the amazing band. I even went out for a while and explored the little town we were in. I went back to my lovely hotel room and had a quick snooze. How many times have you spent a fortune on a hotel room only to feel like you were barely in the place? And if you think that if you disappear for an hour everyone will be wailing into their gin and tonics like they've just watched *Marley and Me*, then you are very much mistaken. No one ever knows you're gone!

Not drinking changes your behaviour but not in a bad way. In fact, you'll probably find a strangely addictive confidence in knowing that you are doing your own thing. For the first time, you're doing what you want when you want to do it. And that's better than any drug.

6. MY SLEEP IMPROVED

This is probably the first thing you'll notice when you take a decent break from alcohol. Booze plays havoc with our sleep quality because when we drink we're asking our body to work through the night. When we're meant to be repairing and recharging, our body is busy processing the alcohol and attempting to bring equilibrium back to our systems. When a drunk person goes to sleep, alcohol withdrawal usually kicks in after about four hours. That's when the anxiety starts, and sleep is always more difficult in that scenario.

Maybe you're one of the lucky ones who doesn't feel like alcohol gives you a restless night. But sleep is so important to my sense of well-being. It's so important for us all. When sleep is affected, everything gets shaky. It's like a caravan caught in a crosswind. It starts to wobble and shake – and you know that the person towing it can do absolutely nothing – until the whole thing eventually flips on its side and bits start to fly off. Sleep regulates our hormones, our moods, our digestion and our performance. If we're constantly throwing a disruptive substance like alcohol into the mix, our sleep will suffer and so will everything else.

In her book *100 Days to a Younger Brain*, neuroscientist Dr Sabina Brennan writes, 'Don't be fooled by the fact that alcohol initially makes you sleepy; it can disrupt sleep later in the night. After a few hours, alcohol acts as a stimulant that interferes with the quality of your sleep. Ditch the nightcap

and avoid drinking alcohol within three hours of bedtime.'
I hit a stage with my drinking where I was just not willing
to sacrifice any more sleep for a few glasses of wine that I
probably wasn't going to enjoy anyway. It's not uncommon
for many of us to have drinks Friday and Saturday and, after
a weekend of compromised sleep, wonder why we're sluggish
on Monday and Tuesday. So, if you've been experiencing
disrupted sleep, have a gentle look at your alcohol intake and
see if a small change could bring the zzzzzzs back ...

7. IT ALLOWED ME TO GATHER MOMENTUM

Nothing kills motivation like a hangover. The night before,
we want to be centre stage. The next day, all we want to do
is hide away and be as anonymous as possible. One of the
reasons I used to feel so bad after drinking was that I felt it
had knocked me off track. Enthusiasm that I might have
had for a project or pastime would suddenly be replaced by
feelings of fear and doubt. Any sense of momentum I felt
I had gained would have to be paused until my emotions
came back on line a few days later and I could get excited
again. It was causing me to lose my 'fizz' for life. I found
this frustrating and it really made me question my motives
for drinking. When I stopped, I found that my excitement
for things could continue because my moods were far more
stable. I felt more rested so I had more energy to devote to
the things I wanted to pursue.

Certainly, we can't stay super-excited about things for-ever and our enthusiasm wanes all the time. But without regularly poking the stick of alcohol into our spokes, we actually get the chance to let things run their course natu-rally, without the stop–start feeling brought on by the dis-traction of a boozy mind. I know in my heart I would never have taken up skateboarding if I had been drinking. (Is that a bad thing? says you.) I would have questioned and sec-ond-guessed myself so much more. The added fear brought on by alcohol would have stopped me from repeatedly risk-ing my neck to get good at it. I would have been more self-conscious for longer parts of the week, so I probably would have avoided sharing my enthusiasm for its playful benefits with other people. I may have tried it but I wouldn't have stayed with it. And I certainly would have missed out on many of the precious weekend skate sessions with my son. And do you know what? It wouldn't have been the end of the world. But how much richer are our lives when we can create the mental and physical space for trying something new and sharing it with the people we love?

8. MY ATTITUDE TO ALCOHOL CHANGED FOREVER

When you decide to try not drinking, it forces you to think. It forces you to think about all aspects of drinking alcohol: the reasons why you drink, the effect it has on you, how you feel before and after drinking, other people's attitudes to your drinking or not drinking, the person you become with alcohol, the person you'd like to be without alcohol. Once you open that Pandora's box, there's no turning back. What emerges is something I had never expected would happen. You become a mindful drinker.

Once you start to question your habit of drinking, it becomes impossible to continue with your automatic and habitual patterns of consuming alcohol. Each time you bring that first drink to your lips, you are practising mindfulness. You are experiencing every aspect of the action, whereas before you were simply letting it go down the hatch. And the questions will keep coming. Why am I doing this? Do I really want to do this? How will I feel tomorrow? How do I want to feel tomorrow? Am I going to have more than this one? Do I even like the taste? Will anyone notice if I stop? It's as if the veil is lifted off drinking alcohol and you start to question every aspect of it and your connection to it. It's a gradual process but, over time, you realise that your relationship with alcohol is changing. It doesn't mean that you change your habits overnight. You may continue in the same manner but it will begin to *feel* different.

It can actually be tinged in sadness sometimes. Weirdly, it can feel like you're losing a friend. Yes, it's one of those friends that you know is a bad influence, but alcohol was there through all the major events of your adult life. You were like soldiers or fellow explorers, mingling together from the most formative of years. It was there when you won and there when you lost. It was the lubricant for awkward conversations and sometimes the fuel for a passionate encounter. It gave you confidence when you needed it and jump-started your sense of humour. For many years, you were thick as thieves. That was, until, you changed.

And now, like a friend who keeps crashing on your couch and dumping their problems on you, it's time to let them go. All those supposed benefits it offered you have just become hindrances, and you're ready to move on. And like any friend that has played a big part in your life, it can be hard to move on from them. There will be times when you are pulled back towards it, when old patterns of behaviour re-emerge and you dive right back in. Over time, however, these instances become fewer and fewer and, before you know it, your old pal alcohol is sleeping on someone else's couch.

I don't see alcohol the same way any more. I don't see it as something I need. I don't see it as a necessary crutch to lean on or an effective way of dealing with my problems. I see it as it really is – a drug that can temporarily take the edge off but that will drag me backwards in the long run. I wouldn't call myself a teetotaller. I'm still open to the idea of having a rare drink with the right person on the right occasion. But I no longer see it as necessary for my happiness, relaxation or peace of mind and, most importantly, I am no longer afraid of life without it.

9. QUITTING ALCOHOL DIDN'T MAKE ME A SUPERHERO

This was another surprising realisation for me. After about six months of sobriety, I began to learn something about myself – I could still be shit *without* alcohol! Many people think on some level, as I did, that if we could just remove alcohol from our lives, we would magically begin to accomplish everything we had put on the back burner for the last 20 years. Guess what? That's not the case. Sure, you may find the enthusiasm, motivation and energy to begin some new, exciting things, but you're never going to do everything. Alcohol can hold us back and numb us from our true selves, but it doesn't stop us being human. The same fears, procrastination, perfectionism, anxieties and periods of self-doubt are still there.

The difference is, however, that when alcohol is taken out of the picture, you begin to see the real personal issues that are holding you back from doing what you want to do and being who you want to be. Up until now, whenever those uncomfortable emotions raised their heads, you immediately reached for something you knew subconsciously would shut them the hell up for a while – alcohol. If a lack of self-belief had influenced the events of your week, chances are you were reaching for a glass of wine or a pint of beer to put those unsettling feelings to bed. Taking a break from booze gives us a chance to get to know the parts of ourselves we've been keeping a lid on for most of our adult lives. It allows us the space to begin to feel real empathy for all the hidden pieces that have been trying to get our attention.

When I stopped drinking, I realised that it wasn't so much the drinking that was making me feel terrible about myself. It was actually my tendency to beat myself up and be hypercritical of everything I was doing. The alcohol was acting as an amplifier for all the negative thoughts I was having towards myself. Through meditation, and giving my brain the space to feel normal over a longer period of time, I began to soften my self-talk until one day I noticed that I was no longer criticising myself like I used to. And when we don't beat ourselves up as much, we don't feel the need to reach for the drug that's going to temporarily silence that behaviour. So, no, you won't suddenly begin learning five languages, you won't become a black belt in karate over-night and you won't climb Everest in your underpants. By reimagining your relationship with alcohol, however, you will begin to reimagine your relationship with yourself, and that's the only one that really matters.

10. MEDITATION IS THE NEW DRINKING!

So, the question is, when you take alcohol out, what do you put in?

How about something that actually relaxes you? Booze doesn't do that – it's a stimulant. You may feel relaxed at the start, but underneath your system is working overtime to keep the car on the road and break down all the sugar and alcohol that's going through your system. Meditation triggers the parasympathetic nervous system that allows your heart rate to slow, your blood pressure to drop and your cortisol and adrenaline levels to fall.

How about something that improves your memory instead of erasing it? Meditation leads to a greater blood flow to the brain, which strengthens the cerebral cortex and boosts memory function. Booze causes you to forget you left the cheesy toast under the grill and burns down your house.

How about something that actually improves your sleep? Meditation lowers the stress and anxiety that can keep us awake. It also boosts production of melatonin, the sleep hormone, and activates the parts of our brain that control sleep. Alcohol disrupts our sleep by triggering our stress response and can also have us going to the bathroom 20 times in one night.

How about something that helps our brains to perform better? Meditation boosts cognitive performance, helps us to focus and lengthens our attention span. Putting the key in the front door can be an insurmountable task after a few pints!

How about something that makes us kinder? Who has more arguments: a person who's just finished a loving-kindness meditation or someone with five white wines on board? Meditation increases oxytocin, the cuddle hormone, and makes us more social, empathetic and kinder to ourselves and others. When it comes to alcohol, let's just say that overnight jail cells ain't full of meditators!

You may at this point be wondering what all the fuss is about. Maybe you have a perfectly healthy relationship with alcohol and think I'm being unnecessarily dramatic. If so, then I am very happy for you. Whatever you're doing, keep doing it! For me, however, and many like me, consuming alcohol causes upset and imbalance. Whatever is happening in my body and brain when I drink is just too disruptive for me to get any real enjoyment out of it. Interestingly, though, a 2019 study from the University of Exeter suggests that people who have high levels of shyness are more prone to the anxiety and fear that arise following alcohol consumption.[34] Could that apply to me? Who knows? Perhaps there is more of that schoolboy who turned purple still in me than I think!

As I said at the start of this chapter, I'm not anti-booze or anti-the people who drink it. I drink it from time to time. But so many of us have learned from a young age that alcohol is the most effective form of stress relief. It's the drug of choice for a lot of homes and this is what we picked up as kids.

It doesn't mean, however, that it is our only option. If you're already feeling that you'd like your relationship with alcohol to change for the better then take comfort in this – the very fact that you are having this conversation with yourself means that things have already shifted. Like it or not, you're already on the path to drinking less or not at all. And adding in something like meditation can be extremely effective in strengthening your resolve and giving you a positive alternative to more destructive forms of stress relief. The best thing is it's free and, unlike alcohol, you can do it at work without punching someone and losing your job. Cheers!

CHAPTER 14

HAPPY BUT NOT HAPPY

I had a conversation in a pub that changed my life. It was three years ago and it came out of nowhere. I was doing my radio show from Cork city, and I travelled down the night before with Dave and the rest of the team. We always head down the night before so we can get settled, have our meetings, plan the show and set up interviews. Well, we say that, but the real reason we go down in advance is we really enjoy hotels without our children. Room service, Netflix and fluffy pillows – what's not to love? Anyway, this particular trip, I wanted to watch the US Masters golf, but as they didn't have it in the hotel, I nipped next door to a bar and pulled up a stool. Pretty soon, I got chatting to a guy who was also into golf.

As with any truly Irish conversation, within minutes we both knew everything about each other's lives. It's something we take for granted here, but an English friend of mine said it was the first thing he noticed about Irish people – the insatiable demand for information. I always just presumed everyone asked loads of questions, regardless of what country you live in. This, however, is not the case. We Irish need to build a profile worthy of an FBI operative before we can accept that the conversation can continue. It's like we must create a context for your entire existence or, at the very least, work out if we know anyone that you know. We think it's normal. Other nationalities find it downright nosey.

Anyway, we were both Irish so the questions flew. He was a Corkonian and had his own architecture business. Things were going well. Very well. In fact, that same day he had signed a contract for a massive building project and his company stood to do extremely well from it. This was partially why he was out having a few pints. He was toasting his success. He was happily married with two beautiful kids and he said he felt extremely lucky.

We got on to the subject of what I did, and it emerged that I was a meditation teacher. He seemed very interested in this and was curious about all aspects of meditation. He said he really needed something and his face began to appear sad. When I asked him what the matter was, he said a sentence that has always stuck with me for its truth and its simplicity. 'I'm happy but I'm not happy.'

He began to admit that, despite having all the things he had wanted from his career and his home life, something was missing. He had ticked all the boxes and reached all the goals that he had believed would bring him joy and fulfilment. Yet here he was, happy but not happy. There's a subtlety to this state of mind that I think is really relatable. He wasn't miserable; he wasn't tearing his hair out or caught up in a desire to change large parts of his life. He was just aware that, whatever path he was on, it wasn't delivering at a deeper level.

For so many people, this is how a desire for change manifests. It emerges from a vague sense that something could be better. We start to become aware that a lot of our time is possibly spent in a state of 'meh'. We experience happiness but not too much joy. We feel successful but not fulfilled. It's something you can't quite put your finger on, but you know somewhere along the way things became fine and didn't move on. Sure, there may be moments of excitement and fun but they don't seem to last very long. Things that used to excite you, like nights out and mad weekends, don't have the same impact and, half the time, you don't have the same interest in them that you used to.

All this can be confusing and at times unnerving because we thought we were on the right path. Just like my friend in the bar, we are told that certain things will bring us joy and fulfilment and that, if we keep the head down and continue ticking those boxes, we will wake up one day and suddenly feel like we've won. We look over the walls of nice houses with gardens and wonder if the people inside feel like they've won. If we've done all the good-job, loving-partner, healthy-kids stuff, then why do we feel like something is missing?

The feeling of being happy but not happy can also bring with it feelings of guilt. We don't want to feel ungrateful. We really appreciate all the wonderful things, people and experiences in our life. But whenever we feel that maybe something is missing, we can experience guilt about being ungrateful, about taking our achievements and successes for granted.

And here is the most important lesson – it's OK to feel these things. It's OK to feel like a passenger in your own life. It's OK to start to question why you do what you do. It's OK to feel happy but not happy. It doesn't mean you're an ungrateful, terrible person who doesn't deserve what they already have. All it means is that you are ready to find some-thing deeper. You are ready to reconnect with that part of you that has been lying silent and waiting patiently while you went about creating an amazing, complex life full of challenges and enriching experiences. You've been busy being a great parent, a great friend, a great son or daughter. You've been taking responsibility and getting things done, all while main-taining and developing relationships, many of which you'll enjoy till your dying day. You've been doing an incredible job!

Now, though, something is telling you that there's room for something else. And this will be the glue that keeps all the other parts together, that puts the wind in your sails and a smile on your face. And the missing piece is – you! The reason you've been feeling that the things and circumstances outside of you haven't been offering the level of joy you yearn for right now is because they are exactly that – outside of you. It took a trip in an ambulance to help me see that filling my day and my world with stuff and jobs was not going to make me feel whole. It would leave me feeling happy but not happy, and the hole that was left would be an open door for alcohol, nicotine, work, sugar and whatever else I felt could fill it with.

It doesn't have to take a near-death experience in Kilkenny to find the missing piece. When we connect with that deeper part of ourselves, which opens up through something like meditation, we start to give meaning to all the things we've been doing so well every day. We don't have to blow up our lives – we just have to allow the wisdom that is already inside of us to guide us the rest of the way. When the nice Cork architect was saying he was happy but not happy, he was saying he had lost touch with himself. And that happens to *everybody*! Why wouldn't it? Look at all the stuff we have to do! We're out there at the coalface just hammering away, working to keep food on the table and the lights on. We're trying to keep fit, look good, be nice and stay positive, often while the goalposts of finances, career and relationships keep moving. As I discussed earlier, the trajectory of our lives is often set in motion by the time we leave school, and we just keep on truckin'. Our winning formula has found its groove and we're playing out whatever software we uploaded years, if not decades, before.

So sometimes, it can feel like we've just woken up on a train. We sit up with a start and wonder where we are and how long we've been asleep. It's perfectly understandable that, with all we've had going on outside and around us, we would lose sight of what's inside. Instead of being something to grow concerned or feel guilty about, realising you're happy but not happy is something to rejoice in. You're waking up! This is where it all begins. You're not replacing anything you've already accomplished – you're giving it substance and depth. You're finally allowing yourself to enjoy the fruits of all your hard work by connecting with the part of you that was actually the driving force behind all you've achieved and overcome. By finding the time to sit in silence and meditate, you're creating room for this longed-for fulfilment to show its face and, pretty soon, you'll be able to really appreciate all you have in your life because it will no longer just represent what's missing. You can start small, a few seconds or minutes a day. Bit by bit, you'll begin to realise that your true self is flooding back in through the very cracks you thought were the problem. And it takes so little for a big change to happen …

A few months ago, I got a message from a chap called Declan. Declan is in his thirties and a father to two young children. He got in contact to tell me something very important – he was singing in the shower. OK, I'd better explain. You see, Declan had been struggling. The pandemic had kicked off and pretty soon after he lost his job. He was doing his best to keep money coming in but work was scarce and his savings were running out. He was experiencing a lot of stress and had difficulty sleeping. What was bothering him the most, though, was his mood. He had become irritable and short tempered. He desperately loved his little family, they were everything to him, but he found that his stress was causing him to be impatient and he was snapping at them. He couldn't seem to relax at home like he used to and was restless and worried. After he was short-tempered with his wife and children, he would then feel very guilty about his behaviour, and he was confused about why he couldn't stop acting that way. He felt like he was letting his loved ones down, and the pressure of that just added to his anxiety.

But there was one thing, in particular, that reminded him that he wasn't himself. He had stopped singing in the shower. This may seem a bit bizarre, but to Declan it was of the utmost importance. For him, singing in the shower is what made him … well, him. He was normally a happy-go-lucky, carefree chap, who didn't fret too much and took everything in his stride. And he sang in the shower every morning. That was his thing. It was a sign that everything was hunky-dory. But he realised that somewhere among the bills and mood swings he had stopped. And it really hit him hard. Where was his old self gone? Where had his everyday joy gone and who was this deflated and stressed version of himself that was struggling to make it through the day?

Then he heard me rabbiting on about the 16-second meditation I had learned all those years ago. He thought, *Well, if that mad lad on the radio does it, it mustn't be too hard*. So he gave it a go. And another. And another. Pretty soon, he was doing it a few times a day. He started to feel better. So he tried my beginners' meditation on my website. He felt even better.

And then it happened. He started singing in the shower again. He was so delighted to start feeling like his old self, he dropped me a line. I was so happy! We chatted over Zoom and he was positively beaming. He explained how, after just two weeks, he had more patience and was way less moody. He was enjoying his family time again, and they were delighted to have upbeat Dad back. Sure, he still had challenges to overcome and problems to solve, but they didn't seem as all-consuming as before. He had more confidence and hope that they were going to work out. Whatever happened, he said, he was going to keep up the meditation and keep singing in the shower.

This story is really important for a few reasons. First, it's a reminder that we are all human. Even the most optimistic and playful of us can get knocked off track sometimes. The reasons may be financial, circumstantial or just bad luck or bad timing. They may be health related or something that's happening in our close personal relationships. Whatever the reasons, our coping mechanisms can be put to the test at the drop of a hat. And we never really know how we're going to react when the volume is cranked up on the stress in our lives. Some people may have a dramatic moment that sets the alarm bells ringing. For others, like Declan, it's a gradual process that takes you away from who you thought you were. Of course, it's not that we're changing as people: we're just reacting to situations in our environment that we haven't quite processed yet.

It can be hard when we feel our emotions are taking over and we're becoming unpredictable. I remember regularly waking up and worrying how the day was going to go, how I was going to react to the people and situations coming my way that day. Because I had no tools at my disposal to manage my stress response, it felt like the day was something that happened *to* me rather than something I was an active part of. As soon as I learned those skills to turn off my inner emergency mode, I started to get back a sense of control. By stepping out of the future and the past and into the present moment, we create the space to look at our lives objectively, without the over-emotional lens that can cloud our perception. The 16-second technique that he used didn't 'cure' Declan of some strange, anxious disease – it merely allowed his body and mind to regroup, to settle, to do the many miraculous jobs they do without the distraction of a stressed-out nervous system. As soon as he turned off his inner alarm, all his cockpit dials returned to normal and he could start to become master of his own inner and outer environments again.

The second thing we can take from this story is something very reassuring indeed: it takes very little to make a huge change. Declan was so surprised that such a small technique could have such a huge impact on how he was feeling. And for many of us, it can be hard to believe that we don't need a major intervention when things start going wrong. Don't get me wrong: for some, a more comprehensive medical or psychological approach is required at times and 16 seconds of breathing ain't going to cut the mustard. But for a lot of us who are experiencing a wobbly period, it can be the smallest of changes that makes a big difference.

My morning meditation changed everything. It reminded me that I had a part to play in how I wanted to feel that day. It reminded me that I wasn't alone, that I had a wise and capable part of me on tap whenever I needed it. All I had to do was breathe and out it came. We're so used to reaching for things outside of ourselves to make us feel better that the idea that we have the resources within us seems just too easy. We want to give someone money so they will just fix it and let us get on with our lives. But we can't get on with our lives until we start to get on with ourselves, and that means taking time to be and breathe with ourselves, even if that's just a few minutes a day.

What this story also reminds us is that we are not broken. Feeling down, anxious, uneasy, restless, irritable, overwhelmed, burnt out, alone, isolated, confused, sad, tired or just plain 'meh' is OK. It really is. It's not forever, and it will pass. I have felt all of those things at some point, sometimes all of them together! And I spent so much time worrying about what was wrong with me. Was this it? Was I ever going to feel normal again? Was there something inside me that had snapped? Of course, there was nothing broken or snapped or falling apart. I just didn't know how to turn off my stress response so I was like a car driving on empty, sputtering and stuttering down the road, veering from left to right.

Being chronically stressed is exhausting. Imagine the old-style town crier running to and fro shouting 'Fire! Fire!' over and over again without a break. The poor chap would collapse after a while. This is what our nervous systems are doing a lot of the time, and we don't even have to be aware of it. Introducing something like a meditation technique can break the cycle of being in a state of high alert and bring us back to ourselves.

It can be hard when you realise that things are getting to you. It's especially hard for people who consider themselves to be generally positive, super-active or high-achieving.

Anxiety, burnout or overwhelm can be seen as something that happens to other people but not to you. So when you find you're suddenly not sleeping and struggling with your thoughts, it can bring on feelings of failure, shame or confusion. No matter how bulletproof we feel, we all need something that allows us the space and energy to recharge. Even Formula One racing cars take time to go to the pits for a tune-up. They can't keep driving around the track indefinitely. If they do, bits start to come off!

So what's your singing in the shower? Is it laughing out loud? Whistling in the car? Playing with the dog? Baking buns? Kicking a ball? Wrestling with the kids? Pinching your partner's bum? Smiling at passers-by? Cracking corny jokes? Whatever it is, it's not silly. It's you. We all have markers or traits that we feel define us at our happiest. When we lose touch with them, it can be upsetting and worrying and seem almost impossible to get them back. But they're always there, waiting to be rediscovered. We just have to create the space for them to reveal themselves. I'm very grateful to Declan for sharing his story with me and now, of course, with you. He's a shining example of 'a little goes a long way' and shows us the journey back to yourself doesn't have to be far at all.

CHAPTER 15

BECOMING THE SAME
BUT DIFFERENT

got my teeth straightened a few years back. When I look back at clips of myself on TV from before then, it looks like I was a national gravel-chewing champion. It's funny how, when you do something like that, *you* forget about it but other people begin to notice something has changed in you. They might not realise exactly what's different but they just know there's an improvement. Beginning a meditation practice often has the same effect. People won't necessarily know that you now make a habit of sitting in silence, turning off your stress response and spending more time in the present moment, but they will begin to see that something has changed. Maybe it's your level of self-confidence, your calmness under pressure or your uplifting mood.

I found that people I didn't even know that well suddenly wanted to confide in me and ask my advice. People began to comment on my general air of calm, which made me laugh. I wasn't necessarily feeling that way all the time! But when you begin to take time out of your day just for you, when you stop allocating all your time to other people, when you make a few daily moments of self-care a priority, something inside you begins to shift. It's almost imperceptible at first but, slowly but surely, the edges become less frayed. Your emotions begin to lose their grip on you and everything starts to feel a little bit lighter. It's the people closest to us who notice this shift first. I asked Dave, my 'work wife', to put into words any changes that he has noticed in me in recent years. This is what he had to say:

'"A changed man" is probably an overused phrase but I've seen it really happen in Dermot over the last few years. Since meditation and mindfulness have become an integral part of his life, the overall contentment level in the man has rocketed. Gone is the self-berating that followed a fun weekend. Gone is the swing in mood that could darken our radio studio. Ups and downs still happen, because we're all human, but how Dermot deals with these is the most impressive change of all. I think this comes from an increase in all types of awareness. Awareness of self, awareness of others and their perspectives, awareness of everything. From the outside, it seems like there is now an ability to "zoom out" of the problem, take stock of the situation from a couple of angles and only give it the attention it needs, rather than allowing it to be bigger than it deserves to be. Our relationship is phenomenal and, regardless of any changes that have come along, I believe it would still be one of the absolute best in my life but, honestly, it makes me so much happier to see the more level, more content, more balanced Dermot of today. Seeing him become a teacher is another element that makes me so proud of him. His communication skills are the best I've ever seen and using these to channel the good message of meditation and mindfulness, knowing the genuine self-discovery behind the teachings, is a wonderful circling of all of his skills. Having any version of Dermot Whelan in my life is one of the key factors in my own overall happiness. It just so happens that this one right now is the best version so far.'

Shut up, *you're* crying! What amazingly kind words from a special man. Although, it does make me wonder … just how painful was I to work with before all this meditation stuff? To see someone so close to me put those changes down in words is quite mind-blowing. But I know it has to be true because best mates will never bullshit you. And I wouldn't be writing this book if I felt you wouldn't see positive changes from the techniques I've outlined.

We've seen what the science says: regular use of meditation can have enormous benefits for your levels of happiness and fulfilment. More than that, though, this new journey that you're embarking on will open you up to so many new possibilities. You'll start to see everything in a new light and gain a profound appreciation for what you already have and what you've already achieved. I remember as a child going on holidays to Lahinch in County Clare. It was the 80s, so going on a summer holiday 40 minutes from your house was perfectly acceptable. When we came back, the house seemed different. It was still our house but, somehow, it had a strange newness to it. I was aware of the smell and the acoustics and the garden seemed bigger. It was familiar and exciting at the same time, even though I had lived there all my life. This is what meditation gives us – a new sense of the old, the ability to see your own life like a rediscovered home. And when we create the opportunity to see ourselves differently, we create the opportunity for real, lasting and positive change.

Sometimes, I think of that guy in the University of Virginia experiment who chose to electrocute himself 190 times. I imagine him sitting there repeatedly hitting the button, and my heart goes out to him. He's just expressing what we all feel a lot of the time. We crave distraction and long to feel something new. Sitting with ourselves and our thoughts can be uncomfortable. All that unfiltered thinking can be noisy and confusing. Listening to our thoughts can be frightening. They can be unkind, erratic and frantic. We can find ourselves fixating on pointless things and avoiding stuff that really matters. It can feel like someone has handed you a broken jigsaw of your personality and you think you'll never be able to find any semblance of order in the whole sorry mess. But with meditation, we keep turning up. Our minds keep wandering and we keep bringing our attention back to our breath. We do our 'I trust's and our 'I am's and we keep closing our eyes and taking a deep breath.

There are days when we feel it's a waste of time and we reach for the TV remote. We drift away from meditation and then we come back and sit down and start again. And the layers begin to peel away. The parts of the jigsaw we thought were most important become the background. A new image begins to emerge from all the chaos and, this time, it's one you really want to look at. Seeing this version of yourself coming alive is as fascinating to you as it is to everyone else. And, one day, you wake up, put your feet on the floor and suddenly realise that you're about to step into a day that's no longer ruled by old habits and destructive patterns of thinking. There's no noisy clamour in your mind and the only thoughts you're aware of are kind and supportive. There is no anxiety about the hours ahead, only a quiet excitement and a powerful sense of calm. This is the life we all deserve: one that's free from angry nuns and ambulances. We can become our own biggest supporters. Our thoughts can be our greatest allies and the person we see in the mirror every day can be our closest friend. So, let's give that friend a fighting chance and create some space for them to be heard. Take it from me – it's better than an unplanned break in Mullinavat …

FAQs

Before you put me down and head off to put the kettle on, here are some answers to questions I get asked a lot.

What's the best time to meditate?
You can meditate at any time of the day and, with the short meditations we learned earlier, you can meditate whenever you're feeling under pressure or a bit overwhelmed. Some parts of the day, however, are more effective than others when establishing a practice that works for you. I recommend the time between waking and reaching for your phone. That's a precious window where the demands of the day haven't yet woken up but you have. It's a wonderful opportunity to set the table for the day and have some input into how you would like it to go. This is where you can check in with yourself and set an intention of how you would like to feel. As weird as it sounds, I feel that the busy, outside 'doing' me and the quiet, inside 'being' me are actually an

amazing team! My meditation is a chance to check in with my partner and reinforce that sense of teamwork. I feel like the 'being' me has my back and vice versa. So when we connect to that inner part of ourselves, we're gathering strength and personal power for the day ahead. If, for some reason, you feel that you are unable to use those few moments after waking for meditation, that's OK. I know lots of parents who like to wait until the kids have left for school and the house is a bit quieter before they begin their meditation. The later we leave it, however, the more chance that our minds are already being pulled in loads of other directions by emails, phone calls, social media and lists of things to do. Find a slot that works for you and keeps you coming back to those moments of silence every day. Remember, now that we know short meditations like belly breathing and the 16-second meditation, the 'I don't have time' excuse doesn't wash anymore! Set your alarm for five minutes earlier and give it a go.

Once you've nailed down the morning meditation and it has well and truly become a habit and part of your daily routine, then you can look at introducing one in the late afternoon or early evening. This is a great opportunity to shake off the mental clutter of the day and set yourself up for an evening of being calm and present. Guided meditations are especially good just before bedtime, as long as you're listening to one designed for relaxation and sleep. You don't want to be listening to a really energising one just before you close your eyes! There should be a perfect one for you in my special guided meditations available to all readers on my website www. dermotwhelan.com with the code MINDFULL21.

How long should I meditate for?

My advice is start small. Sometimes, with the best of intentions, we can try to bite off more than we can chew in the early days and we're not able to sustain it. Some beginners attempt to do half an hour or an hour straight out of the gate and it's too much. It's like beginning an exercise programme that is too intense too quickly. We'll get disheartened and tired and won't keep it up. If you can turn up every day for five minutes of listening to your breath, then start there. If you can repeat your 'I trust' mantra silently in your head for seven minutes, go with that. If you manage to do a ten-minute guided meditation, then do that every day. Whatever length of time works for you and keeps you turning up for yourself, stick with that. Then, when you have that locked in, try doing a few minutes more. But, remember, it's not a competition and longer does not necessarily mean better. It has to be a time that you feel you can manage daily and truly connect with. The more you do it, the more time you will want to spend in that space, so let it develop naturally.

Where should I meditate?

Somewhere comfy! As impressive as the lotus position looks on Instagram, it's not necessary. For many of us, those intense poses can leave us with aching knees and dead legs. If we find somewhere comfortable and warm, like a favourite chair, a cosy couch or even sitting up in bed, we are far more likely to come back and do it again. I have a comfy two-seater couch in my man-cave that I like to use. If I'm feeling like I might fall asleep, I also have a little meditation stool I use that keeps me in the kneeling position but without giving me pins and needles! Some people like to use a meditation cushion or wrap themselves in a blanket. Finding your own ritual is a nice part of it all and creates a kind of 'sacred space' that's just for you. The beauty of meditation is, of course, that you can take it anywhere. I've meditated in trains, planes, buses, cars, in airports, shopping centres, forests, fields, offices, backstage dressing rooms, toilets and even radio studios! If you find yourself with a few minutes to kill, just start to focus on your breath or repeat your mantra and, suddenly, what used to be boredom or mindless scrolling on your phone is now a precious moment of brain and mood enhancement. And the best part is, no one has to know what you're doing!

Should I listen to music while I meditate?

A lot of guided meditations already have music on them and that's OK. Many of mine that are available on my website have music on them. It can often act as a helpful cue to our subconscious that it's time to find a more relaxed state. Some people, however, see it as more distraction and another expression of our need to escape the discomfort of silence. Again, I believe in whatever works for you. If you find in the early stages that music is a necessary part of the experience for you, then go with it. You may find later that you're ready to introduce more moments of pure silence into your day. When we're looking for the right piece of music, it can end up taking up our precious meditation time as we fiddle around with Spotify or YouTube. Then an advert comes on and scares the hell out of us! Sometimes, it's just simpler to sit in silence.

What should I be experiencing when I meditate?

As humans in a busy world, we are very goal-oriented. It's hard to approach anything without having a specific desired outcome. So vague ideas like 'allowing' or 'witnessing' can leave us feeling like we're doing it wrong or that it's not worth doing. In fact, it's the opposite. When we are able to engage with something like meditation without expecting any particular outcome, we allow the benefits to unfold naturally. Just as a sheet hanging on the washing line isn't trying to get dry – it merely rests there in the wind and getting dry is the outcome. (I hope you don't mind me comparing you to laundry!) When we meditate, we are putting ourselves into a space where our bodies and minds can find equilibrium, where our nervous systems can settle and healing can take place. We are creating the environment for inner change, which will then manifest as outer change.

There is no particular way you are meant to feel after meditating. Some days, you will get up from your meditation feeling calm and peaceful. Other days, you might feel emotional, spaced, grumpy or sleepy. Whatever you're feeling, just know that it is merely a snapshot of what's happening in your conscious and unconscious mind at that particular time and that it will pass. If you have deep spiritual experiences when you are sitting in silence, or you see colours or feel all kinds of weird and wonderful things, then that's fantastic. If you experience nothing other than a strong desire to scratch your nose and eat chocolate then that's fine too! It's all about just turning up and finding the silence.

What do I do if meditation brings up uncomfortable thoughts or feelings?

This can happen when we begin to sit in silence. It's not that meditation is creating those thoughts or feelings, it's just that we're finally giving them the opportunity to be heard. It's kind of like walking into your garden shed for the first time in years. As you open up the space, you'll witness all sorts of things that have been hidden away in there. We don't have to engage with any of those thoughts as they arise; we just acknowledge that they are there and allow them to pass through. It's really helpful if we can apply a kind of playful curiosity to what arises. So if we experience a thought or feeling about a parent, for example, we would merely think to ourselves, *Oh, that's interesting, I'm having a thought about my mother. It doesn't feel very good. I seem to be feeling it in my gut. I'm just going to let it do what it needs to do. Now, I'll just bring my attention back to my breath.* Uncomfortable feelings can cause many of us to shy away from meditation sometimes. But this is very much the time to keep turning up. Meditation allows us the opportunity to witness what's happening beneath the surface and, if something keeps presenting as an issue, it can point us in the direction of seeking more thorough help from an expert or therapist. I have often felt very emotional after a meditation session. In the beginning, I was worried that I was making myself worse and that the meditation was making me sad. What I later realised was that these moments in silence were allowing some old feelings of discomfort to come to the surface. So I just said to myself, *OK, feelings, you do what you need to do to pass on through and I won't get in your way.* If I felt weepy, I'd just go into my bedroom and let it out. If I felt irritable, I'd just accept what I was feeling and try to give those around me a heads up! Pretty soon, the big waves of emotion became smaller waves until the inner sea was a whole lot calmer. So if you are experiencing a lot of emotion when you meditate, you're not doing it wrong. Just stay curious about what's coming up for you and let it pass through. If it feels too big to deal with on your own, reach out for help and let someone guide you through the process.

Why does my mind keep jumping all over the place?

Because we've never trained it to do otherwise! One of my favourite videos on YouTube is of a dog show. It's a very big affair and all the finest and rarest dog breeds are there with their proud owners. The event featured in the video is an obstacle course for dogs with various hoops, tunnels and the like that the dogs are required to run through. It is also, however, littered with treats and toys that any dog would love. The test is if the dog can ignore the distractions and complete the course. The competition begins and all of the beautifully behaved dogs carry out the tasks flawlessly. That is, with the exception of one. A golden retriever takes to the track and is clearly very excited to be there. His tail is wagging, his tongue is hanging out and he begins to run and jump all over the place. Much to the embarrassment of his owner, whose instructions are falling on fluffy but very deaf ears, the retriever ignores every task and instead eats the snacks, plays with the toys and has the time of his life. He is bounding from one feature to the next and is utterly oblivious to the whole competition. Eventually, he has to be chased down by several officials, and the red-faced owner leads him away. It always makes me laugh and you just can't help rooting for the dog in the midst of all that snooty canine seriousness!

As well as being a very entertaining video, it's also a great analogy for our minds. Just like the golden retriever, our minds are in the habit of wandering all over the place and following any distraction that comes our way. Even when our logical side is doing its best to keep things organised, the giddy, curious part of our brain wants to head off in all kinds of directions, even if it's counterproductive. Through a meditation practice, we gently train our minds to become a little more focused. Science shows regular meditation lengthens our attention span and boosts our ability to focus on one thing for longer.[35] So the more we meditate, the easier it becomes, as we activate and strengthen the parts of our brain that help us to behave less like a crazy golden retriever and more like a well-behaved best friend. It's not just the quality of our meditation that improves. When we develop the ability to focus for longer and experience less mind-wandering, we are not as likely to be distracted in all aspects of our life. We find it easier to stay focused on our goals, and we spend less time on people and things that aren't aligned with our deeper sense of purpose. A negative news story or an anxious conversation is not as likely to disrupt our emotional wellbeing. We begin to foster a greater sense of self as we are less influenced by the people and situations around us. There's a crazy puppy in all of us, but it doesn't mean we have to let it rule our thoughts and emotions. So, when you realise your mind has wandered, just say 'Good doggy' and return to your breath!

Why do I keep forgetting to meditate?

Because you're human. The best way to ensure you don't forget to meditate is to make it a routine. We are creatures of habit and tend to do things in the same order each morning. If we can build our morning meditation into that routine, it becomes second nature and we barely have to think about it. More than that, it feels wrong if we don't do it. They say it takes 21 days to establish a habit. Whatever the number, give yourself a chance to let it become something that just happens and you'll never look back. Use technology to help you remember. Set reminders and alarms on your phone or ask your smart speaker to remind you. Leave Post-its on your computer or paint one fingernail a different colour – whatever works! Most importantly, though, if you do forget, don't use it as another excuse to be hard on yourself. Just get back on the horse and start again.

Is meditating once or twice a week enough?

Put it this way – if you went to the gym every now and again, would you get the 'beach bod' you were looking for? All the science shows that the real changes take place in the brain when we meditate regularly. Ideally, that means every day. We want that amygdala to shrink and the volume to be turned down on those anxious, fearful and angry thoughts. The brain is a muscle like any other part of the body. The more we work it, the greater the results. Once or twice a week is fine if all you want is an occasional sense of relaxation. If you want real, tangible effects that will help balance your emotions, improve your sleep and increase self-reliance, then jump in every day.

Can my kids do it?

Yes! Most children are very open to the idea of meditation. For them, mindfulness is their natural state, and they can exist in the present moment for hours without even thinking about it. In my experience, the best way to engage them is to lead by example. When they see you taking time out to listen to a guided meditation or sitting in silence with your eyes closed, their curiosity will get the better of them. They will want to know more and will want to see what it's all about. Try it together and let them experience it first-hand. Initially, they may not stay for the whole thing, but that's all they need. They may do a bit longer the next time. Bedtime is a great time to introduce it as it can quickly become a calming and settling cue for bringing on sleep. My daughter is nine years old and loves to listen to a guided meditation at night. She usually lasts about a minute before nodding off! Kids also love the ritual around meditation, so comfy cushions, candles, dim lighting and relaxing music can all be great ways to get them to engage with it.

Don't force it, however. If they're not interested now, they may engage with it at a later date. What's important is that you show them that it's perfectly normal to take time out for ourselves in our busy day, and that there are tools they can reach for when their emotions are troubling them. Why not try the Family Meditation available on my website?

How do I get my partner to do it?

I meet a lot of people who really want someone close to them to try out meditation. It can be frustrating when someone we love is experiencing stress and we know that something like meditation could help them. If they're not open to the idea, badgering them is just going to make them feel worse. The best tool you have is to lead by example. When the people around us see the positive benefits of a meditation practice manifesting in us, they are far more likely to become curious and try it for themselves. Remember, our ripple is a very powerful thing and it will move out into all parts of our life. When you are shining brighter, those around you will notice.

If someone close to you is resistant to trying meditation or any other stress-relieving practice, be patient with them. They are just operating from the level where they find themselves right now and may feel fearful or awkward about this whole space. If meditation is a step too far at the moment, then maybe suggest taking some time out in nature, watching a comedy or getting some exercise. When we're feeling burnt out or stressed, taking on something new can seem even more challenging. Elevating our mood and confidence through other means can often create the space for new ideas and experiences to take root. In the meantime, breathe for two!

Which is better – a breath or mantra meditation?

It's really up to you. Try them both and see what you think. Personally, I find it easier to focus on a mantra (a syllable, word or phrase that you repeat silently in your mind). You may like to mix it up and change it day to day. Just try to stick to the same technique within the one meditation. Pick a style and commit to it for the session. Otherwise, with all the chopping and changing, you can start to lose confidence in your practice.

Are guided meditations useful?

Yes, particularly for beginners. I see them as the personal trainer of meditation. If you've ever joined a gym, you know that those early days can be daunting. We're suddenly exposed to lots of techniques and information and it can become a bit confusing. The personal trainer takes us under their wing and helps us to relax and navigate the new environment so we can find our groove. A guided meditation is very similar. A teacher guides us through the experience so we can slide over into the passenger seat and enjoy the ride. There may come a time, like in the gym, when you want to go on your own a bit more. You will be more familiar with the techniques and have a good idea of what resonates with you. You can then try more sessions with just yourself in charge. I like to mix it up and do guided ones from time to time – especially at bedtime, as I find they can really set me up for sleep and help me to unwind. So try out all the methods and see what works for you.

Why do I keep falling asleep when meditating?

Think about it. We've trained our bodies and minds into a certain way of operating. Closed eyes? Sitting or lying down? Slower breathing? It must be time for sleep! And our inner computer shuts the system down. When we meditate, we teach our systems another state to enjoy: closed eyes, sitting or lying down, slower, deeper breathing *but* an alert mind. That's meditation! Over time, we get used to that state and our body knows not to activate sleep mode unless we really, really need it.

Of course, there is another reason why you could be falling asleep – YOU'RE TIRED! Very often, those few minutes of meditation in the day could be the first time you've actually sat down and relaxed. Generally, we can go through a whole day without ever taking a break, and the first time we actually take a deep breath and relax is the moment our head hits the pillow at bedtime. No wonder we're tired! So if you do find yourself falling asleep in the beginning, don't worry. Just let yourself get some of the rest that your body obviously needs. I'm a big fan of the power nap! If it continues to be an issue for you, try finding a position for meditation that makes it a little harder to fall asleep. Consider using a meditation stool or cushion instead of a couch or armchair. Try to avoid using a bed for meditation and definitely try to avoid meditating lying down unless you're trying to fall asleep.

How do I know if it's working?

If you're turning up for your meditation each day, it's working. Science tells us that. It's quite normal, however, to wonder if it's having any effect in the beginning. If you really want to see if it's working, meditate every day for two months. Then stop. You'll definitely notice how much it has been helping you! It's a lot like exercise. We may not be aware of the benefits we're getting from exercise until we stop. Then we realise that it was actually really helping our mood and energy. Meditation is the same. You'll only fully appreciate the positives when you stop doing it altogether. So, my advice is … don't stop!

What's a good meditation for getting to sleep?

As I mentioned earlier in the book, sleep was a big deal for me. Broken sleep was the first sign all those years ago that something was not right. When I learned the right tools to turn off that stress response, my sleep immediately improved. One major reason for sleep disruption is that our stress response is still firing and stress hormones, like cortisol and adrenaline, are still buzzing around our system. We cannot enter the rest-and-digest state if our inner alarms are still ringing. Introducing a simple breathing technique can often be enough to calm our nervous systems long enough for us to fall asleep. This is why the military use these techniques in the field to enable them to sleep under very challenging conditions. So I recommend the following if you are trying to get to sleep or trying to fall back asleep after waking:

- belly breathing (page 134)
- 16-second meditation (page 137)
- body scan (page 146)

Each of these is very effective at firing up the parasympathetic nervous system and allowing the process of sleep to take hold. Also, meditation naturally boosts our levels of melatonin and helps us to bring our focus into the present moment. When we're not ruminating on things that have already happened or worrying about things that might happen in the future, our 'thinky' mind can relax and sleep can take over.

What if it's just not for me?

Sometimes, people can feel this way. It can seem like everyone else gets it but, for some reason, it just isn't clicking for you. If you experience this, don't worry – you won't be expelled from meditation school! Give it time. It's a new skill that you're learning and no one feels like an expert straight away. Think about it. How could sitting with your own thoughts be for other people and not you? How could breathing be something that only other people can appreciate? The inner, calmer version of you is only dying to meet you, so don't throw in the towel just yet. It's the most natural thing in the world to sit in silence with ourselves. The busy world we live in, however, can make it feel like the opposite is true. Remember the scientific study where people chose to electrocute themselves instead of sitting alone with their thoughts for fifteen minutes?

Everyone finds it challenging to venture into the silence of their own mind. Sometimes, it can feel like an uncomfortable place. But the truth is we're just out of practice. When you were a child, you spent hours in the space between your ears, guided only by imagination and a sense of play. You can get there again. All you need is some patience and an understanding that you've got everything you need waiting for you in those moments of silence you carve out of your day. Remember, start small. If a mindful walk is all you can muster at first, then do that. If 16 seconds is all you can do before the discomfort gets too much then that's OK. You'll soon find everything begins to get easier and electrocuting yourself is the furthest thing from your mind!

Can exercise be meditation?

It's certainly true that there are elements of exercise that can be mindful and very beneficial. I like to think of mindfulness as those moments that you're so immersed in the present that you lose all track of time. I've often been out for a run and found a kind of meditative groove where my breathing falls into a natural, repetitive rhythm. I'm not worried about anything and I feel like I could keep going and going forever. These are special moments and exercise can really lift our spirits and enhance our mood. Exercise, however, is another 'doing' activity in our already busy day. There's nothing wrong with that, but it's also important to make room for the 'being' moments as well. That may sound a bit Yoda-ish, but if we're trying to find more calm and turn off that stress response, sometimes a noisy gym or spin class may not be the ideal place. Intense exercise can raise our cortisol and adrenaline levels and, if we're already in a stressed state, we may not get the relief we need. Of course, enjoying meditation or exercise should not become an either–or situation. They can complement each other enormously, and this is why most elite athletes have some form of mindfulness or meditation practice to strike the right balance. So enjoy your exercise, allow those mindful moments to fuel your sense of wellbeing and allow the quiet moments of meditation to be the perfect preparation for your next physical challenge. Now you can put the kettle on ...

NOTES

1   Richard Knox, Patti Neighmond, 'Stressed Out: For Many Americans, Stress Takes A Toll On Health And Family,' National Public Radio (NPR) (7 July 2014)

2   Fiona Brennan, *The Positive Habit: Six Steps for Transforming Negative Thoughts into Positive Emotions*, Gill Books (2019)

3   Fritz Strack, et al., 'Inhibiting and facilitating conditions of the human smile: A nonobtrusive test of the facial feedback hypothesis,' *Journal of Personality and Social Psychology*, 54(5), (1988)

4   '42 Worrying Workplace Stress Statistics,' The American Institute of Stress (AIS) (25 September 2019)

5   Julie Ray, 'Americans' Stress, Worry and Anger Intensified in 2018,' Gallup (25 April 2019)

6   Abiola Keller, et al., 'Does the perception that stress affects health matter? The association with health and mortality,' PubMed Central (PMC) (31 September 2012)

7   Britta K. Hölzel, et al., 'Mindfulness practice leads to increases in regional brain gray matter density,' PubMed Central (PMC) (10 November 2010)

8   Nadia Whitehead, 'People would rather be electrically shocked than left alone with their thoughts,' ScienceMag.org (3 July 2014)

9   Matthew Hutson, 'People Prefer Electric Shocks to Being Alone With Their Thoughts,' *The Atlantic* (3 July 2014)

10 'Former UNC Students Report Mindfulness Meditation Helps Relationships,' EurekAlert! (7 February 2005)

11 Jennifer S. Mascaro, et al., 'Compassion meditation enhances empathic accuracy and related neural activity,' *Social Cognitive and Affective Neuroscience*, Volume 8, Issue 1 (January 2013)

12 Christina Zelano, et al., 'Nasal Respiration Entrains Human Limbic Oscillations and Modulates Cognitive Function,' PubMed Central (PMC) (7 December 2016)

13 Luciano Bernardi, et al., 'Effect of rosary prayer and yoga mantras on autonomic cardiovascular rhythms: comparative study,' PubMed Central (PMC) (22 December 2001)

14 James Nestor, *Breath: The New Science of a Lost Art*, Riverhead Books (2020)

15 Jim Flick and Jack Nicklaus, 'Jim Flick and Jack Nicklaus: Go To The Movies,' *Golf Digest* (27 April 2010)

16 Daniel Rapaport, 'How Tiger Woods stays locked on his target when hitting through crowds,' *Golf Digest* (26 October 2020)

17 Teresa Heiland and Robert Rovetti, 'Examining effects of Franklin Method metaphorical and anatomical mental images on college dancers' jumping height,' *Research in Dance Education* (January 2012)

18   Vinoth K.Ranganathan, 'From mental power to muscle power—gaining strength by using the mind,' *Neuropsychologia*, Volume 42, Issue 7 (3 February 2004)

19   Muhammad Ali, Richard Durham & Toni Morrison, *The Soul of a Butterfly: Reflections on Life's Journey*, Simon & Schuster (2004)

20   Alan Richardson, 'Mental Practice: A Review and Discussion Part I,' *Research Quarterly, American Association for Health, Physical Education and Recreation*, 38:1 (17 March 2013)

21   Xianglong Zeng, 'The effect of loving-kindness meditation on positive emotions: a meta-analytic review,' PubMed Central (PMC) (4 November 2013)

22   Elizabeth A. Hoge, et al., 'Loving-Kindness Meditation practice associated with longer telomeres in women,' PubMed Central (PMC) (August 2013)

23   Wendy M. Johnston, Graham C. L. Davey, 'The psychological impact of negative TV news bulletins: The catastrophizing of personal worries,' *The British Journal of Psychology* (The British Psychological Society) (13 April 2011)

24   Shawn Achor, Michelle Gielan, 'Consuming Negative News Can Make You Less Effective at Work,' Harvard Business Review (14 September 2015)

25   Shunryu Suzuki, *Zen Mind, Beginner's Mind*, Shambhala Publications (1970)

26   Jon Kabat-Zinn, *Wherever You Go, There You Are: Mindfulness meditation for everyday life*, Hyperion (1994)

27   Charles Y. Murnieks, et al., 'Close your eyes or open your mind: Effects of sleep and mindfulness exercises on entrepreneurs' exhaustion,' *Journal of Business Venturing*, Volume 35, Issue 2 (March 2020)

28   Troels W. Kjaer, et al., 'Increased dopamine tone during meditation-induced change of consciousness,' *Cognitive Brain Research*, Vol. 13, Issue 2 (April 2002)

29   Patricia Sharp, 'Meditation-induced bliss viewed as release from conditioned neural (thought) patterns that block reward signals in the brain pleasure center,' *Religion, Brain and Behavior* (September 2013)

30   Lynn Barnett, 'The Playful Advantage: How Playfulness Enhances Coping with Stress,' *Leisure Sciences* (March 2013)

31   Dr Sabina Brennan, *100 Days to a Younger Brain*, Hachette (2019)

32   Prof. David Nutt, *Drink?: The New Science of Alcohol and Your Health*, Hachette (2020)

33   Prof. David Nutt, 'Alcohol alternatives – a goal for psychopharmacology?' *Journal of Psychopharmacology* (1 May 2006)

34   Beth Marshab, 'Shyness, alcohol use disorders and 'hangxiety': A naturalistic study of social drinkers,' *Personality and Individual Differences*, Volume 139 (1 March 2019)

35   'Meditation helps increase attention span,' ScienceDaily, Association for Psychological Science (16 July 2010)

ACKNOWLEDGEMENTS

Thank you to my beautiful wife, Corrina. Thank you for your calm, your never-waning support and belief and your incredible art that lights up our world. You're so interesting, and I love you to bits.

Thank you to Rosie for your fun, excitement and uncompromising independence.

Thank you to Matthew for your enthusiasm for creating amazing art and contagious love of silliness.

Thank you to Owen for your never-ending curiosity and creativity. Keep the random facts coming!

Thank you, Buddy, for being the emotional Polyfilla for my wonderful family.

Thank you to Niamh T, Niamh Mc, Andy, Noel and all the amazing NK Management team for your incredible support and advice every day.

To Sarah, Aoibheann, Teresa, Ellen, Linda and all at Gill Books, thank you for taking a chance on me and guiding me every step of the way.

To Siobhán McKenna, thank you for giving me that first meditation lesson! You literally changed my life!

Thank you to Siobhán Sheehan for your wonderful healing, supportive chats and for knowing I would write this long before I did!

To my teacher, Davidji. Thank you for investing so much time and energy in me and all your other students. For your continuing support, knowledge, meditations, guidance, humour and that 'first sip of a pint of Guinness' voice! Big love, my friend.

To my radio team, Dave, Maria, Eimear, Cathal and Séan, for allowing me to indulge my creative craziness on a daily basis. You guys rock.

To Cillian for writing such beautiful words. May we meet and laugh at nonsense soon!